SINS OF SILENCE

STORIES OF THOSE

WHO ACT IN THE FACE OF INJUSTICE

AND THOSE WHO REMAIN SILENT

William A. Beckham

2nd Edition

July 10, 2020

HISTORICAL AND PERSONAL STORIES FROM SLAVERY AND SEGREGATION

I dedicate these stories to my Grandchildren and their Children, and Children everywhere, who are learning to speak and live courageously in a world that often does not hear, see, or speak in the face of injustice. May God write His ethical stories through their lives and touch the hurting through them. May God speak through them His kindness and compassion.

"Though seeing, they do not see;
though hearing, they do not hear or understand.
In them is fulfilled the prophecy of Isaiah:
'You will be ever hearing but never understanding;
You will be ever seeing but never perceiving.
For this people's heart has become calloused;
They hardly hear with their ears,
And they have closed their eyes.
Otherwise they might see with their eyes,
Understand with their hearts and turn,
And I would heal them.'
But blessed is your eyes because they see,
and your ears because they hear.'
Jesus: Matthew 13:13-15

PREFACE

"Listen for the silence . . . . because it is there."
William A. Beckham

In the face of injustice why do some act and others remain silent? This is the nagging question I have asked over and over about my own life and about people in general. It is the motivation for this little book.

Of course, both personal ethics and social ethics are part of the answer to the question above because one cannot exist without the other. Social justice flows out of personal integrity and real personal integrity expresses itself in social justice.

Jesus pointed out the inconsistency of some people about ethics. A person can meticulously keep personal ethics down to the most minute rule about food, but "neglect" social ethics: "the weightier matters of the law: justice and mercy and faith" (Matthew 23:23). Someone can also advocate for social ethics and justice and be devoid of personal ethics.

My intent is to better understand what actually motivates someone (you and me) to personally reach out beyond self-interests and to see, hear, touch, and speak for the defenseless, diminished, ignored, oppressed, and hurting.

Stories

The heart of this book is a group of simple stories that have ethical themes and truths. These stories give a human face to academic ethics and illustrate the personal pain of injustice. The stories tell me that Kindness and Mercy are qualities that are always present when the silence is broken and when someone acts in the face of injustice.

I have chosen stories that touch hearts and minds where both good & evil, and courage & cowardice, find shelter and lodging. I have intentionally limited the amount of commentary about the ethical lessons in order for each story to speak its own truth to each reader.

In these stories, we meet people who speak out in the midst of social crisis and those who are silent. These ethical reactions live side by side in the same circumstances, in the same periods of history, in the same families and communities, and often in the same stories. The stories remind us to act in a moral way within the hard context of social problems and the harsh reality of our own weaknesses.

In some of these stories, the beauty of ethical living starkly contrasts unspeakable horrors, unthinkable circumstances, and ugly persecution. These stories clearly show the personal price required for speaking and the human cost for being silent in the face of injustice. Both extraordinary and ordinary events and people form these stories. Holocaust survivor, Eli Zborowski, saw a puzzling mystery about who speaks and who remains silent in the face of injustice. "My Father was killed by Poles, but I was saved by Poles. It really shows that you can never generalize about people."

These are not all "feel good" stories that provide easy and comfortable answers. In fact, some of the stories may raise additional questions about why some people remain silent and some speak out in the face of the personal pain and suffering of others.

History

At a fund-raiser for the John F. Kennedy Presidential Library in 1985, President Ronald Reagan personalized history when he said, "History is not only made by people, it is people." In speaking about the slain president, Reagan reveals a lot about his own view of good and evil in history. "He (JFK) had written a book as a very young man about why the world slept as Hitler marched on, and he understood the tension between good and evil in the history of man --- understood, indeed, that much of the history of man can be seen in the constant working out of that tension."

In a Wall Street Journey article (July, 2020) and on television, Cardinal Timothy Dolan recently shared a great insight into society and history. "Society must have memories and dreams." Indeed, the tension of good and evil in life and history operates between the poles of memories (our past) and dreams (our present and future).

The history-defining "I Have a Dream" speech of Dr. Martin Luther King Jr., delivered at the Lincoln Memorial on August 28, 1963, is obviously built upon both memories and dreams. Dr. King understood the importance of both retaining the memories of past history and pursuing the dreams of future history, even the painful memories and far away dreams. He knew if we cut one from the other, we cannot survive.

Therefore, the stories in this little book are about both memories and dreams. The memories are about some who were silent and about some who acted fairly in the face of injustice. The dreams are about a world of justice, equality and fairness.

These stories are part of history from its ethical people perspective. History is people and people live within the context of good & evil and memories & dreams. In the tension between good and evil, we all leave an ethical footprint in the journey of history.

World War II, Slavery and Segregation in the United States are periods when history was filled with "tension between good and evil." Ethical heroes and villains walk together through these historical moments, sometimes side by side and sometimes as the same person. These three periods of history illustrate the challenge of speaking out during explosive and even dangerous social upheavals.

History has already judged the actions of Hitler, the evilness of the institution of slavery, and the senselessness of segregation. Reflections on these stories may help us personally explore our real attitudes about injustice and to evaluate our ethical actions and inactions in the present.

I don't presume to speak for Jews in the first set of stories because their suffering is too personal and painful for a non-Jew to try to explain. The Holocaust museums around the world tell their stories and the Nation of Israel is a living reminder of their struggle.

I have no personal context for understanding their suffering, but I know about the silence. More than anything else it was the silence that allowed the violence against the Jews. It was the silence that inflicted the pain, fear and indignity. Silence allowed the suffering.

The same is true of the second set of stories from the period of slavery and segregation. I cannot speak for the anguish and agony of Black Americans, but I can speak to the destructive indifference because I was part of a culture and a church that remained silent and ignored the problem and the pain.

In some stories about segregation, I share a slice of my own early memories. These personal stories are to remind the next generations that social choices are part of ordinary living by ordinary people in times that appear ordinary. We all have connections to the ethics of the past; we all have opportunities in the ethics of today; and we all shape the ethics of tomorrow through our children and those we influence about good and evil. We live out both memories and dreams.

Silence

While searching for answers about injustice, I continually ran into a wall of silence. It became obvious to me that injustice and silence are the flip sides of the same coin of indifference. Edward Yashinsky was a Yiddish poet who survived the Holocaust only to die in a communist prison in Poland. He understood first-hand the evil consequences of silent indifference.

> *Fear not your enemies, for they can only kill you.*
> *Fear not your friends, for they can only betray you.*
> *Fear only the indifferent, who permit the killers and*
> *Betrayers to walk softly on the earth.*

(Reference in Lookstein Haskel: *Were We Our Brother's Keepers?* New York: 1985.)

These stories from World War II, slavery and segregation tell how some reacted with courage and some with silence in the face of injustice. These stories remind us that silence is never a solution or an option in the face of injustice.

So, as you read these stories, listen for the silence . . . . . because it is there, in the far and near past and in our present.

WHY DO SOME ACT AND OTHERS REMAIN SILENT?

INTRODUCTION

SILENCE IS VIOLENCE

"Silence is Violence" was the message on the T-shirt worn by Ivy, a 28-year-old Canadian woman who sat in the window seat on our flight from London to Toronto. I discovered she was a committed activist with a heart to help the poor organize into co-ops in order to improve their lives. Amnesty International distributed the shirt as a protest about the violence against women around the world.

The slogan, as most slogans are, is overly simplistic, but true. Silence shares in the sin that it ignores. Therefore, silence shares in the violence, in the injustice, in the hate, in the prejudice, in the suffering, and in the oppression of Man. Silence is an effective tool of Satan that increases the intensity of suffering and evil and ignores the hurting, helpless, and weakest in society. Personal silence in the face of social wrongs is a primary cause of much of the injustice and misery in the world.

Is God Silent?

On the very day I met Ivy and read the caption on her T-shirt, newspapers around the world carried a story about Pope Benedict XVI. The pope was on his first official visit to the Nazi concentration camp at Auschwitz, Poland. At that evil place, the Nazis systematically killed 1.5 million men, women and children, mostly Jews. On Sunday, May 28, 2006, after praying at the cells and crematories, Pope Benedict called the visit "particularly difficult and troubling for a Christian, for a pope from Germany."

Silence was a central issue during his visit to Auschwitz. Reporters reopened the painful questions about the silence of Pope Pius XII and the Church during the time of the Holocaust. Pope Benedict added to this theme of silence in the words he spoke that were carefully recorded by the accompanying press corp.

"Words fail," said Benedict. "In the end, there can only be a dread silence, a silence that itself is a heartfelt cry to God." "Why, Lord, did you remain silent?" he said, his voice wavering. "How could you tolerate this?" He said he came "as a son of the German people, a son of that people over which a ring of criminals rose to power by false promises of future greatness and the recovery of the nation's honor, prominence and prosperity, but also through terror and intimidation."

Pope Benedict's words about the silence of God raise perplexing theological and ethical questions. Benedict voices the rhetorical questions that Mankind asks God. "Why, Lord, do you remain silent?" and "How can you tolerate this?" These questions may be the anguished and legitimate cry of the soul in the midst of terrible suffering and injustice. However, Adam and Eve used these same type questions to shift blame back to God for their own sin. We are genetically programmed as their children to use this same technique. The assumption is that God's silence either means He doesn't love or doesn't have the power to use that love to protect us. Both assumptions are self-serving attempts to escape personal responsibility for our actions and inactions.

One reporter observed that while the Pope "spoke eloquently about forgiveness and reconciliation, he did not beg pardon for the sins of Germans or of the Roman Catholic church during World War II. He laid the blame squarely on the Nazi regime, avoiding the painful but now common acknowledgment among many Germans that ordinary citizens also shared responsibility." (See, Benedict in Auschwitz, Ian Fisher, The New York Times, Wednesday, May 31, 2006.)

The truth of the matter is, Humans have the silence problem, not God.

The Long Silence

Toward the end of WWII, a group of prisoners in Auschwitz actually conducted a mock court in one of the barracks. They appointed a judge, selected a prosecuting attorney, designated a defense attorney, and chose a jury. God was the defendant on trial for their terrible ordeal. Many witnesses angrily testified about the terrible crimes and injustices they suffered. The verdict? God was found guilty for allowing the inhuman crime of Auschwitz.

John Stott captures this same understandable but misplaced anger toward God in a story called *The Long Silence*. The surprising ending shows that in Christ God enters into the suffering, pain, injustice, and silence in the world. (*The Cross of Christ*; John Stott, p336f.)

> *At the end of time, billions of people were scattered on a great plain before God's throne. Most shrank back from the brilliant light before them. But some groups near the front talked heatedly, not with cringing shame, but with belligerence.*
>
> *"Can God judge us? How can he know about suffering?" snapped a pert young brunette. She ripped open a sleeve to reveal a tattooed number from a Nazi concentration camp. "We endured terror. . . beatings . . . torture . . . death!"*
>
> *In another group a Negro boy lowered his collar. "What about this?" he demanded, showing an ugly rope burn. "Lynched . . . for no crime but being black!"*
>
> *In another crowd, a pregnant schoolgirl with sullen eyes, "Why should I suffer" she murmured, "It wasn't my fault."*

Far out across the plain there were hundreds of such groups. Each had a complaint against God for the evil and suffering he permitted in his world. How lucky God was to live in heaven where all sweetness and light, where there was no weeping or fear, no hunger or hatred. What did God know of all that man had been forced to endure in this world? For God leads a pretty sheltered life, they said.

So each of these groups sent forth their leader, chosen because he had suffered the most: A Jew, a Negro, a person from Hiroshima, a horribly deformed arthritic, and a thalidomide child.

In the center of the plain they consulted with each other. At last they were ready to present their case. It was rather clever. Before God could be qualified to be their judge, he must endure what they had endured. Their decision was that God should be sentenced to live on earth . . . as a man!

"Let him be born a Jew. Let the legitimacy of his birth be doubted. Give him a work so difficult that even his family will think him out of his mind when he tries to do it. Let him be betrayed by his closest friends. Let him face false charges, be tried by a prejudiced jury and convicted by a cowardly judge.

Let him be tortured.
At the last, let him see what it means to be terribly alone.
Then let him die.
Let him die so that there can be no doubt that he died.
Let there be a great host of witnesses to verify it."

As each leader announced his portion of the sentence, loud murmurs of approval went up from the throng of people assembled. And when the last had finished pronouncing sentence, there was a long silence.
No one uttered another word.
No one moved.
For suddenly all knew that God had already served his sentence.

Walk with me through these stories. We may see ourselves in some of them, and we may even see God.

STORIES OF COURAGE AND SILENCE
FROM THE JEWISH HOLOCAUST

WE ALL HAVE AN ETHICAL STORY!

"History is not only made by people, it is people."
Ronald Reagan

WHY DO SOME ACT AND OTHERS REMAIN SILENT?

STORY 1

A Beautiful German Village

It is necessary only for the good man
to do nothing for evil to triumph.
Richelieu (act III, sc. 1, l. 49)

While teaching a conference in Germany, I visited a beautiful little village that touched me deeply. Burghaun, in the state of Hesse, has a population of several thousand people. A huge compound is one of the most prominent landmarks in the village. Catholic and Protestant Churches in varying forms have occupied parts of the compound during its long history. Among other things, the compound has housed a hospital, an orphanage and a center for the homeless and destitute. Additional buildings were constructed within the compound to facilitate the changing purposes of the complex. An imposing stone fence surrounds the buildings.

A Village Chapel

At some point, a partition wall was built at the end of one of the largest buildings in the compound. The result was a lovely little chapel that seats several hundred worshippers in two separate seating sections. Each Sunday, even during World War II, the Protestant villagers passed through the front gate of the compound on the way to worship. Catholics worshipped in a nearby building. Hedges obstructed the view into the other parts of the compound and restricted contact between villagers and the inhabitants. Inside the chapel, a large black door in the partition wall was the only access to the rest of the huge building.

When Hitler first came to power in the 1930's, the compound was used as a holding center for political prisoners such as Communists, Democratic Socialists, Jehovah Witnesses, Homosexuals, Gypsies and Jews. Detailed records tell the human story and tragedy that followed. Jews and other "undesirables" from the surrounding regions were systematically arrested, sent to the facility and processed for eventual assignment to the death camps. This included all of the 114 Jews who lived in the little village at the beginning of the war. Not a single Jew remained in the village by the end of 1942. A few villagers protested the plight of the Jews and were also arrested. This suggests that the people in the village knew something wrong was going on in the restricted areas of that compound.

At the beginning of Hitler's rise to power, the political prisoners in the compound were marched into the little chapel through the black door and forced to worship on Sunday with the people from the town. As the oppression continued, the door was locked and the villagers were cut off from the prisoners for the duration of the war.

In order to accommodate the increasing number of prisoners, the vast space in the part of the building beyond the little chapel was remodeled into several floors with rooms and holding cells. On the opposite side of the chapel partition wall, cells with chains anchored into the walls can still be seen. Prisoners who survived the concentration camps remember hearing the sounds and songs of worship on Sunday coming from the church.

As I stood in that deathly quiet building, I realized if the prisoners could hear the villagers then the villagers could surely hear the prisoners. However, these villagers had no ears to hear sounds beyond the chapel, no eyes to see what was going on beyond the walls or hedges, no voices to ask about the disappearance of their neighbors, and no hearts to show compassion.

Memories of the Pastor's Daughter

The daughter of the Burghaun Protestant pastor sheds some light on the village and the Jews. She was a young child when her father was pastor between 1931 -1950. Her oldest brother was killed at the age of twelve in an Allied bombing raid at a nearby train station in 1944 while on his way to school. In spite of the war and the death of her brother, she has warm memories of the village of her childhood. After several decades, she moved back to Burghaun and set out to establish a memorial for the Jews who had lived in the village.

When she sought to discuss the Nazi period of history, the response of her parents and older residents surprised her. Her mother began to weep and the daughter charitably concluded that her mother had been so busy with family duties that she didn't know what was going on. Her father also seemed to remember few details about the Burghaun Jews. She painfully concluded that even though her beloved father "had not personally dirtied his hands" he had not "dared much on behalf of the Jews either."

In one of their last conversations before his death in 1991, he revealed a deep inner anguish about the Jews, but still shared few details. He expressed his feelings by saying: "We all failed the Jews," and as if he wanted to reinforce his statement he repeated, "We all failed the Jews!"

This daughter was conflicted with her love for her parents and hometown and the facts of what happened there. "Whereas I was reared well protected in my parental home and my father proclaimed the 'Good News' of Jesus the Jew from Nazareth, numerous Jewish children and their families from Burghaun had been 'picked up' and murdered in the extermination camps of the Nazis, and I had not heard anything about it, unfortunately not even from my parents. Nevertheless I did love the village of my childhood, a place surrounded by fields, meadows, and rolling hills. However, to realize later on what kind of a tragedy had occurred in that place was very painful, and it didn't let go of me ever again. I felt a deep obligation as a member of the former pastor's family to explore and research this suppressed chapter of town history."

What Would I Have Done?

A few days after visiting the village of Burghaun I traveled to Frankfurt by train. On that trip I experienced a flashback to a time of more than five decades. In my mind, I could see the Nazi uniforms, the patriotic signs and officials checking registration papers. The scene playing out in my mind looked like an old-World War II movie. On that trip through the beautiful countryside a heavy feeling came over me, and a question kept nagging me.

The question was not about how the Germans could have allowed the evil of Hitler and Nazism to control their country. I certainly did not feel morally superior to the villagers at Burghaun. The disturbing question that haunted me was: "What would I have done if I had lived in that little village at that time?" Would I have paid the price to make ethical and moral decisions no matter what the cost? Would I have had the eyes to see, the ears to hear, the heart to feel, the voice to speak, and the courage to oppose if faced with the same personal, social, political, economic and religious costs?

Why Do Some Act and Others Remain Silent?

STORY 2

Metropolitan Kyril: A Bulgarian Village

Whether thou goest, I will go.
Your people will be my people,
and your God will be my God!
Metropolitan Kyril

A relatively small percentage of the population in Germany actually participated in either the planning or execution of Hitler's plans at their most evil levels. However, a much larger number was silent about the evil and looked the other way. Daniel Jonah Goldhagen classifies both groups as "Hitler's willing executioners" and uses that phrase as the title of his painfully disturbing book.

In the book, Goldhagen includes an intriguing map (page 413) of Europe during World War II. In the middle of each country is listed the number of Jews murdered in that country during the Holocaust. For instance, 134,500 – 141,500 Jews were killed in Germany. The most Jews were killed in Poland: 2,900,000 – 3,000,000. The second greatest number was killed in the Soviet Union: 1,000,000 – 1,100,000. In Bulgaria, "0" was the surprising number of Jews listed as killed during the Holocaust.

All 50,000 Jews in Bulgaria survived because King Boris, the Bulgarian Parliament, and the people of Bulgaria protected them from being sent to the death camps in Poland.

Tony Campolo tells the story of an event in a Bulgarian village that may help explain why no Jews were killed in this country that was under Nazi control. This particular Bulgarian village faced many of the same choices as the Burghaun village in the previous story: Nazis, Jews, and concentration camps. However, the response and results were vastly different.

Metropolitan Kyril

"One of the most amazing stories to come out of World War II concerns a church leader in Bulgaria named Metropolitan Kyril. When the Nazis rounded up the Jews in his city and herded them into a barbed-wire enclosure, he decided to act.

The train that was supposed to take the Jews to Auschwitz pulled up at the station. The S.S. guards were just about ready to load the Jews into the box cars that would take them to the gas chambers when suddenly, Metropolitan Kyril appeared. He was a tall man to start with, but as an Orthodox priest, he wore a miter on his head, which must have made him appear like a giant as he emerged out of the darkness. He was wearing his black robes and his white beard hung over them. Marching behind him were many of the townspeople. Kyril went to the entrance of the barbed-wire enclosure, which was then surrounded by his supporters. When the Nazi guards tried to stop him, he laughed at them and pushed aside their guns. He went in among the Jews and as they surrounded him, crying hysterically, he raised his hands. He quoted one verse of Scripture, and with that verse he contributed significantly to the changing of the destiny of a nation. Quoting from the Book of Ruth he declared to his Jewish friends, "Whither thou goest, I will go. Your people will be my people, and your God will be my God!"

The Jews cheered and the Christians joined in cheering. They were no longer separate peoples. They had become one in the declaration of the Word of God.

Because of such heroics, not a single Bulgarian Jew ever died in a Nazi concentration camp during World War II, in spite of the fact that Bulgaria was controlled by the Nazi powers. When a man is willing to lay down his life to oppose oppression and injustice, amazing things can happen." (*Let Me Tell You a Story*, Tony Campolo, p133-135; W Publishing Group; A division of Thomas Nelson, Inc.)

Ethical Heroes

Why was Metropolitan Kyril willing to confront injustice while the citizens of Burghaun were deaf, blind, dumb and numb? What was in his mind as he walked up to those soldiers and pushed aside the rifles? How was he able to stand up to the power of the Nazi government and army? What motivated him to act courageously? What internal factors and forces drove him to risk his life? How could he defy the political and military forces? This is the puzzling dilemma about ethical behavior, or the lack of it.

If we find the answer to these questions then we have discovered the secret of ethics because ethics is not about the mind to understand the theory of ethics but about the courage of applying ethics in life. Ethics are always defined at the point of some kind of gun and threat of death.

Metropolitan Kyril and his villagers were ethical heroes because they risked their own lives for the sake of people doomed to an unjust death. They were so overwhelmed by the mercy, justice, love and power of God that it poured out in selfless action. The powerful compassion of God overcame the primal fear of personal danger. This kind of ethical courage is driven by the righteous justice of God that speaks and acts against injustice no matter what cost. God's moral compass becomes more powerful than the danger of the external forces of power.

WHY DO SOME ACT AND OTHERS REMAIN SILENT?

STORY 3

ANDRE TROCMÉ: A HUGUENOT VILLAGE

We do not know what a Jew is, we only know men.

Pastor Andre Trocmé

During the winter of 1940-41, a Jewish woman fleeing Nazi persecution arrived in Le Chambon-sur-Lignon, France. Chambon, a Huguenot village of 5,000 Christians, is located 350 miles from Paris in the rugged mountains of south-central France. The desperate woman knocked at the door of Andre Trocmé, the Protestant pastor, and he warmly welcomed her into his home. By 1942, Jews throughout Europe were following her path to Chambon.

For Jews in those years, this small village in France was perhaps the safest place in all of occupied Europe. The French farmers and shopkeepers in Chambon rescued Jews from the Holocaust in the largest communal effort of its kind in Europe. The faith and conscience of the village was so strong they willingly risked their own lives to protect a group of people who had been labeled disposable outsiders.

The French Vichy government collaborated with the Nazis in allowing 83,000 French Jews, including 10,000 children, to be sent to Nazi concentration camps. Only 3,000 ever returned. In stark contrast, the villagers in Chambon, armed with their Huguenot faith, saved the lives of 5,000 Jewish refugees. Every home in the village hosted at least one Jewish refugee and not a single Jew was betrayed in four years.

Huguenots knew what it was like to be the victim of government injustice and abuse. They were Protestants driven out of Catholic France in the 17th century. The first allegiance of Huguenots was to God's kingdom and not to the earthly powers that were often the agents of oppression. Therefore, over the years they had become experts at survival.

Some Huguenot hiding places in the area of Chambon were hundreds of years old. Every family was an observation post and their dogs for centuries had warned of danger when strangers or soldiers entered the village area.

Andre Trocmé

Andre Trocmé, the pastor of the Protestant church, was born in 1901 from a long line of Germans and Huguenots. Trocmé was a committed pacifist and the moral compass for Chambon. He and his church were committed to living out Jesus' Sermon on the Mount and that meant loving God and loving one's neighbors.

The day after the French Vichy government signed an armistice with Germany, Pastor Trocmé instructed his church about Christian dissent. "The duty of Christians is to resist the violence brought on their consciences, through the weapons of the spirit." When the deportation of Jews from Paris began in 1942, he spoke out in another sermon. "The Christian Church should drop to its knees and beg pardon of God for its cowardice."

When France fell to the Nazi invasion, Pastor Trocmé already had his own solution for protecting Jews from the Nazi's "final solution" of the death camps. Refugees were welcomed and the village fed, clothed, and sheltered all who were in need. Jews were housed in private homes, on farms, and in public institutions. Special "safe houses" were provided within the heart of Nazi-controlled France. When the Nazis came searching for Jews the citizens of Chambon hid them in the countryside. In addition, Trocmé organized an industry of false passports and identity papers and developed a well-organized underground railroad to Switzerland and Spain.

Pressure

The national leader of the Reformed Church in France pressured Trocmé to stop helping Jews because it put the other Protestant churches in danger. Trocmé refused.

The Vichy authorities continued to demand that the pastor cease his activities with the Jews. He replied: "These people came here for help and for shelter. I am their shepherd. A shepherd does not forsake his flock. I do not know what a Jew is. I know only human beings."

In the summer of 1942, two Vichy French police buses arrived at the village. The police captain demanded that Andre Trocmé give a list of the Jews being sheltered in the village. The demand was accompanied by the threat of arrest, but the pastor refused to give up the names. The next day the buses left without prisoners. One of the villagers later recalled: "As soon as the soldiers left, we would go into the forest and sing a song. When they heard that song, the Jews knew it was safe to come home."

As the Nazis gained tighter control of the puppet Vichy government, they demanded more forcefully that the pastor and the people of Chambon turn over all Jewish refugees. The Nazis were flabbergasted that a group of ordinary citizens would defy them over people not even their family. They could not understand why these simple villagers protected Jews.

Eventually, Trocmé was arrested along with a number of the villagers. However, he was released after a few weeks, without signing a commitment to follow government orders regarding the Jews. Daniel Trocmé, his cousin, died in a Nazi death camp. After his release, Andre Trocmé himself was forced to hide from the Nazis for the duration of the war. The pastor's wife, and other women in the village, then coordinated the rescue of the refugees.

Voices of the Village

Pierre Sauvage was born in Chambon in 1944. He grew up in the village with little awareness of his Jewish heritage or the history of the village. Sauvage received an Emmy for his documentary film about Chambon.

Weapons of the Spirit was released in 1989 after five years of what the director called "much soul searching." Sauvage was not prepared "for the character of the Chambon people. They had such a bedrock sense of values that it shook me to the core." Sauvage explained that the church and its pastors sparked a "conspiracy of good" in opposing Nazi policies. In an interview about the documentary, he reflected that the story of Chambon is "a banister kids can hold onto while looking at evil in this world. If we don't feel deeply that we are capable of good, we will be reluctant to face the extent we are capable of evil."

Pascal Blanc, a real estate agent in the village rejected the label "heroic" for the villagers. "It was normal for us to help. We have helped all the time in our past. This is who we are."

A writer asked another villager about the motivation for their goodness. "How can you call us 'good?' We were doing what had to be done. Who else could help them? And what has all this to do with goodness? Things had to be done, that's all, and we happened to be there to do them. You must understand that it was the most natural thing in the world to help these people."

An old villager later recalled: "We didn't protect the Jews because we were moral or heroic people. We helped them because it was the human thing to do."

Why Do Some Act and Others Remain Silent?

STORY 4

Dietrich Bonhoeffer: Ethical Struggle

Only by living completely in this world
do we learn to have Faith.
Dietrich Bonhoeffer, *The Cost of Discipleship*

Dietrich Bonhoeffer was born in Germany in 1906 into a prominent German family. His career as a theologian, writer, and teacher was centered in Berlin, his boyhood home. Bonhoeffer studied at Union Theological Seminary in New York City under the American theologian, Reinhold Neibuhr. While in New York he attended and taught Sunday School at Abyssynian Baptist Church in Harlem and greatly admired the free worship he saw there and the songs he heard. Upon his return to Germany he introduced Negro Spirituals and Gospel songs to his students and friends.

Bonhoeffer's life intersected the same general time-and-place continuum of Adolph Hitler. While in prison in 1925-1926 Hitler wrote Mein Kampf, *My Struggle*. Hitler's personal and political struggle produced some of the most horrible ethical transgressions that the modern world has ever witnessed. In stark contrast, Bonhoeffer's struggle was an inspiration to thousands within Germany during one of the evillest times in history. Even after 75 years his example continues to encourage all who know his story.

Confrontation

Hitler became Chancellor of the Nazi Party on January 30, 1933 and Bonhoeffer was one of the first to publicly criticize him. In 1934, at the young age of 27, he broadcast a message to German pastors on "The Church and the Jewish Question." He boldly urged the pastors to "stand with the Jews." The broadcast was cut off the air before Bonhoeffer could complete the address. Later Bonhoefer wrote to a friend that regarding the Jews "the most sensible people have lost their heads and their entire Bible." (Page 109, *Hitler's Willing Executioners*.)

Between 1934 and 1939 Bonhoeffer made several trips abroad and each trip presented him with a personal decision about returning to German. By 1939 the handwriting was on the wall about the intentions of Hitler. The Swiss theologian, Karl Barth, had been expelled from Germany, Martin Niemoeller, the most prominent pastor, had been placed in a concentration camp, and hundreds of pastors were put in prison. Through contacts in the German Intelligence, Bonhoeffer knew of the planned horror of the Holocaust. That year Bonhoeffer visited friends in the United States. However, he soon felt that he had to return to Germany. He asked the question, "Where am I needed?" and made the statement that "he who believes does not flee."

Bonhoeffer returned to Germany in September of 1939 and formed an underground community of seminary students. They experienced *life together* in community, and that is the title of one of his last books. He also became involved in the German Resistance Movement. Thereafter, community with God and his students sustained him in his struggle in and out of prison.

Last Days

On April 5, 1943, after a plot on Hitler's life, the Gestapo arrested Bonhoeffer's brother-in-law, Rudiger Schloeicher, for conspiracy. Bonhoeffer was also arrested by the Gestapo in the house of his parents along with his sister Christel and her husband, Hans von Dohnanyi. He was interrogated and tortured. Over the next two years he was imprisoned in several concentration camps.

The prison guards were deeply moved by Bonhoeffer's loving spirit and ministry to the other prisoners. They provided him with scraps of paper on which he wrote his letters and thoughts and helped smuggled them out of prison. These thoughts from prison formed the bulk of his last books that are treasured today. The *Cost of Discipleship* challenged the church to renounce "cheap grace" and to live out God's real grace in sacrificial living. His desire toward the end was to finish his book, *Ethics*. Bonhoeffer believed ethics was based on the will of God, not on right and wrong. His thoughts about ethics give a special perspective to the question of what a pacifist does while living in an evil society. While writing on ethics, he opposed an unjust government even to the point of participating in plans of violence. His little book, *Life Together*, gives a New Testament view of Christian community while he lived in clandestine community with a group of his students.

On October 5, 1944 he was transferred from Tegel Prison to the main Gestapo (German Intelligence Agency) prison at the Prinz Albrechstrasse in Berlin for his execution.

One of the last messages received from him was a poem composed at the Gestapo prison in Berlin during very heavy air raids. It was entitled *New Year 1945* and includes the following prophetic and poetic words:

> *Should it be ours to drain the cup of grieving even to the*
> *dregs of pain, At Thy command, we will not falter,*
> *Thankfully receiving all that is given by thy loving hand.*
> Collier Books; Macmillan Publishing Company; NY.

In February of 1945, the Gestapo prison in Berlin was destroyed by an Allied air raid. Consequently, Bonhoeffer was taken to the concentration camp of Buchenwald and to other places until he arrived at Flossenburg. An English officer who was a prisoner at Flosenburg wrote about the last days of Bonhoeffer.

> *Bonhoeffer always seemed to me to spread an atmosphere of happiness and joy over the least incident and profound gratitude for the mere fact that he was alive. He was one of the very few persons I have ever met for whom God was real and always near. On Sunday, April 8, 1945, Pastor Bonhoeffer conducted a little service of worship and spoke to us in a way that went to the heart of all of us. He found just the right words to express the spirit of our imprisonment, the thoughts and the resolutions it had brought us. He had hardly ended his last prayer when the door opened and two civilians entered. They said, "Prisoner Bonhoeffer, come with us." That had only one meaning for all prisoners—the gallows. We said good-by to him. He took me aside: "This is the end, but for me it is the beginning of life."* (Preface to *Life Together*.)

The text on which he spoke on that last day was "With his stripes are we healed." The next day, just days before the liberation of the camp, he was executed by hanging by the SS Black Guards on the special orders of SS chief Heinrich Himmler. He was 39 years of age. This happened about the same time as the execution of his brother Klaus and his sisters' husbands, Hans von Dohnanyi and Rudiger Schloeicher.

Bonhoeffer's body has never been recovered, but a plaque in the village church near his place of death commemorates his life with ten words: "Dietrich Bonhoeffer, a witness to Jesus Christ among his brethren."

WHY DO SOME ACT AND OTHERS REMAIN SILENT?

STORY 5

Martin Niemoeller: The Nightmare of Silence

*The world is a dangerous place to live, not because
of the people who are evil, but because of the
people who don't do anything about it.*
Albert Einstein

Martin Niemoeller was one of the most respected Protestant church leaders in Germany when Hitler came to power. A decorated U-Boat captain in the First World War, Niemoeller became a well-known Christian pastor in charge of a prestigious suburban parish in Berlin. Hitler saw him as a major threat to his Nazi policies even though in the beginning Niemoeller primarily opposed Hitler's attack on the church. Only later did he oppose Hitler's broader political policies against the Jews.

In 1933, Niemoeller, as leader of the Pastors' Emergency League, became the most influential German voice against Hitler. This Church Synod denounced the abuses of the dictator in a famous document called the "Six Articles of Barmen." Niemoeller negotiated with Hitler in an attempt to convince the Nazi dictator to allow the Church in Germany to remain open. Hitler became more and more enraged as Niemoeller and the church group continued to confront him about the abuses of his policies. When Niemoeller preached a sermon entitled: *God is my Fuehrer* (God is my ruler) Hitler's German Youth bombed his home.

34

Niemoeller's leadership in drafting the "Six Articles of Barmen," his personal confrontations with Hitler and other visible joint actions and sermons finally led to his arrest on July 1, 1937. An honest judge let him go with a lenient judgment. However, Hitler rescinded the judgment and personally ordered him jailed. Niemoeller was in concentration camps, including long periods of solitary confinement for eight years, until the end of the war.

Niemoeller's Famous Quote

After the war, Niemoeller was active in international church affairs and made speaking trips across the United States. At that time he brought a message of confession about the blindness and silence of Christians and the Church as Hitler rose to power and implemented his "Jewish final solution." He was haunted by the failure of the Church to deal with the evil State that destroyed the ethical and moral foundations of Germany.

Niemoeller will always be remembered for his quote about the danger of ethical silence in the face of social injustice.

> *First, they came for the communists,*
> *and I did not speak out -*
> *because I was not a communist;*
>
> *Then they came for the socialists,*
> *and I did not speak out -*
> *because I was not a socialist;*
>
> *Then they came for the trade unionists,*
> *and I did not speak out -*
> *because I was not a trade unionist;*
>
> *Then they came for the Jews,*
> *and I did not speak out -*
> *because I was not a Jew;*
>
> *Then they came for me -*
> *and there was no one left to speak out for me.*

I first heard Niemoeller's quote in 1952 when Miss Parsons read it to my Eighth Grade English class. Most of our Fathers and Uncles had left home a decade earlier in order to stop Hitler who was the "they" in the disturbing quote. The words of Niemoeller hit me in a powerful and personal way that day. The quote tested my faith as a young Christian and my courage as a thirteen-year-old. I remember wondering for the first time: "Would I have had the courage to speak out."

Niemoeller's Nightmare

In a March 1946 lecture in Zurich, Martin Niemoeller confessed: "Christianity in Germany bears a greater responsibility before God than the National Socialists, the SS and the Gestapo. We ought to have recognized the Lord Jesus in the brother who suffered and was persecuted despite him being a communist or a Jew." He concluded: "Are not we Christians much more to blame, am I not much more guilty, than many who bathed their hands in blood?" (*Hitler's Willing Executioners,* 114.)

Tony Campolo shares an interesting aspect of Niemoeller's struggle. "Toward the end of his life, Niemoeller told of a recurring dream that he had in which he saw Hitler standing before Jesus on Judgment Day. Jesus got off of His throne, put his arm around Hitler, and asked, 'Adolph! Why did you do the ugly, evil things you did? Why were you so cruel?'"

Hitler, with his head bent low, simply answered, "Because nobody ever told me how much You loved me."

The bishop reported that at this point in the dream he would wake up in a cold sweat, remembering that during the many, many meetings he had had with Hitler, he had never once said, "By the way, Fuhrer, Jesus loves you! He loves you more than you'll ever know. He loved you so much that He died for you. Do you know that?"

So often we fail to bear witness, and hence lose precious opportunities to alter the course of history."

Let Me Tell You a Story, Tony Campolo, 108; W Publishing Group; A division of Thomas Nelson, Inc.

WHY DO SOME ACT AND OTHERS REMAIN SILENT?

STORY 6

OSCAR SCHINDLER: WHY DID HE DO IT?

The path to Auschwitz was paved with indifference.
Ian Kershaw, Christ's College, Cambridge

The movie, *Schindler's List*, is the story of Oscar Schindler who saved more than 1100 Jews during World War II from Nazi concentration camps and death. These Jews worked in his wartime ammunition factory and were on a list of people he protected. Eventually he smuggled every person on the list out of Nazi controlled territory.

The question about Schindler that even Jews ask is "Why did he do it?" Why did he spend something like 4 million German marks keeping his Jews out of the death camps? At the end, why did he risk his life to rescue these Jews from the train to Auschwitz?

When Schindler started using Jewish workers, they were just a way to keep his factory operating so he could make money. He did not mistreat them, but neither did he go out of his way to save them from their ultimate fate. Gradually his motives changed and he actively sought to protect his workers from their ultimate fate with the Nazis.

We identify with Oscar Schindler because we see an ethical evolution in his life that gives us hope. Schindler's story shows his wandering ethical journey that we so often travel. In Schindler's journey, we see our own imperfect struggle with making right ethical decisions when society around us permits and even perpetrates injustice.

The story of Oscar Schindler is an example of the power of humanizing and personalizing people. These people went from being Jews, to being his workers, and finally to being real people. They became "his" Jews.

Steps in Schindler's Ethical Journey

Schindler's ethical journey began at the point of *disinterest, detachment and indifference*. He was not particularly interested in the Jewish issue in one way or the other. He didn't act against the Jews. He was just intellectually detached from the issue and chose to be emotionally neutral. In the beginning Schindler was simply blind to oppression and injustice.

As his factory project got under way, Schindler acted according to *self-interest*. He felt good when he could increase his wealth and influence while helping some people. Schindler operated at a shallow level of ethics we see today. Tax credits are given for helping the poor and self-serving actions give a façade of caring.

Schindler's contact with Itzhak Stern, his Jewish factory supervisor, helped him put the situation into a deeper ethical context. He began to approach the ethical issue of the Jews from a *moral code of behavior*. "Do unto others as you wish others to do unto you." Schindler began to do what was right because he had been taught to do what was right.

At a certain point Schindler entered the ethical zone of *human compassion*. The plight of the Jews touched his heart and compassion spilled over toward them. He began to identify with his workers. Some Germans were anti-Semitic but felt compassion for the plight of the Jews. Compassion is an essential component in Schindler's ethical transformation.

Finally, something of God's *sacrificial and unconditional love* began to operate in Schindler. Schindler's list was actually a real list written by Stern with ink on a sheet of paper. However, Stern and the other Jews knew that the list was really written by God with the love, compassion and kindness that had developed in the heart and soul of Oscar Schindler during his ethical journey.

One More

Schindler's ethical transformation can be seen in a dialogue in the movie. Schindler and Itzhak Stern are having a final conversation in Germany as the workers are boarding a train to escape. Schindler is overwhelmed with regrets when he thinks about how many more Jews he could have saved.

Schindler: I could've got more . . . I could've got more, if I'd just . . . I could've got more.

Stern: Oscar, there are eleven hundred people who are alive because of you. Look at them.

Schindler: If I'd made more money . . . I threw away so much money, you have no idea. If I'd just . . .

Stern: There will be generations because of what you did.

Schindler: I didn't do enough.

Stern: You did so much.

Schindler: This car. Commandant Goeth would've bought this car. Why did I keep the car; ten people, right there. Ten people, ten more people . . . this pin, two people. This is gold. Two more people. He would've given me two for it. At least one. He would've given me one. One more. One more person. A person, Stern. For this I could've gotten one more person and I didn't. I didn't . . ."

A Pile of Stones

A powerful final scene in the movie jumps forward several decades. Survivors on the list and their decedents gather at the simple grave of Oscar Schindler. One by one, each person places a small stone on Schindler's grave symbolizing a special connection and appreciation. The impressive pile of stones represents the lives of 1100 people and their descendants. These people at his graveside were alive because Schindler slowly developed eyes to see, ears to hear, and a heart to feel the plight of injustice of his Jewish workers. To this day, the stones testify to his ethical journey.

As I watched this moving scene, I wondered . . . . will I have any stones testifying to my ethical journey?

Why Do Some Act and Others Remain Silent?

STORY 7

Irena Sendler: The Warsaw Ghetto

You cannot separate people based on their race or religion.
You can only separate people by good and evil.
The good will always triumph.
Irena Sendler

Irena Sendler was born in 1910 in Otwock, Poland, fifteen miles southeast of Warsaw. Her grandfather led a rebellion against the Czars. Her father was a physician who raised her to respect and love people regardless of their ethnicity or social status.

When a typhus epidemic broke out in 1917, he contracted the disease and died while caring for his poor Jewish patients. His dying words to seven-year-old Irena, his only child, were: "If you see someone drowning, you must jump in and try to save them, even if you don't know how to swim."

Irena exhibited a strong social conscience. At Warsaw University in the 1930s, she deliberately sat on the Jewish side of a classroom. When the teacher told her to move, she declared, "I'm Jewish today." The university expelled her immediately.

As a young woman, Irena "jumped in" during World War II and rescued 2,500 Jewish children in Poland from almost certain death. She convinced Jewish parents and grandparents to entrust their children to her because they were in danger of dying in the Warsaw Ghetto or in the death camps. She smuggled the children past the Nazi guards and then adopted them into the homes of Polish families or hid them in convents and orphanages.

Social Worker and Underground Agent

In 1939, when Germany occupied Poland, she was a senior administrator in the Social Welfare Department of Warsaw. In charge of soup kitchens located in every district of the city, she distributed meals, financial assistance, and medical services to the poor, elderly and orphans. Irena ignored the anti-Semitic laws and included the Jews in her welfare programs.

Hitler's plans to liquidate the Jewish population were already in place by 1940. The Nazis herded more than 500,000 Polish Jews into a small sixteen-block area known as the Warsaw Ghetto. Five thousand Jews were dying each month in the deplorable conditions. As a social worker, Irena received a special permit to visit the ghetto area at any time in order to combat contagious diseases. This gave her the opportunity to provide many Jews with clothing, medicine, and money. Dressed in a nurse's uniform to distract the soldiers and wearing a Star of David armband to assure the Jews, she boldly walked through the ghetto streets.

As the situation in the ghetto deteriorated, Irena focused on saving the children. In an interview, Sendler explained: "When the war started, all of Poland was drowning in a sea of blood. But most of all, it affected the Jewish nation. And within that nation, it was the children who suffered most. That's why we needed to give our hearts to them."

The Children

Irena Sendler became an expert in smuggling Jewish children out of the Warsaw Ghetto. She was one of the most effective operatives in Zegota, the Polish underground resistance movement. Irena recruited at least one person from each of the ten centers of the Polish Social Welfare Department to pass along hundreds of false identity papers and documents with forged signatures good enough to fool the German authorities. Each child had a fictitious birth certificate, a baptismal record and a family history of parents, siblings, aunts and uncles that the children, if old enough, had to memorize. They learned the Catechism and Christian songs because the Gestapo drilled children suspected of being Jewish. Irena placed them in secure homes with non-Jewish families, orphanages or convents where they could live safely with new identities. She recalled: "I sent most of the children to religious establishments." "I knew I could count on the Sisters." "No one ever refused to take a child from me."

Sendler later recalled distraught parents asking. "Can you guarantee they will live?" She would reply frankly: "No." "I can only guarantee they will die if they stay."

Irena and her group smuggled children out in ambulances and hid them in trunks and suitcases on the trolley. They sedated smaller children and carried them out in potato sacks, boxes, body bags, or coffins. Sewers, underground tunnels and the courthouse were escape routes. Some got out through a church at the edge of the ghetto with two entrances. A child entered the church from the ghetto side as a Jew and exited the other side as a Christian. Once on the outside, her group might relocate a child several times in order to escape detection. She recalls carrying a little boy from one guardian family to the next, as he sobbed, "How many mothers can a person have? This is my third!"

Sendler carefully recorded the children's original names and their new identities in code on thin cigarette or tissue paper.

She buried this information in glass jars in a friend's garden under an apple tree near the Warsaw Ghetto. Her intention was to return the children when possible to their parents, or at least to let them know who they had been. Sendler's jars contained the names of 2,500 children.

Prison, Torture, and Death Sentence

For two years, Irena's covert operations were undetected. In 1943, SS chief Heinrich Himmler ordered fellow SS officers to complete "the extermination of the Jewish people." The Nazis could only accomplish this demonic mission by the disposal of the large number of Jews already collected in the Warsaw Ghetto. Therefore, the full weight of the power and evilness of the Nazi organization came upon that place and any person standing in their way.

The owner of one of her meeting places divulged her name to the Gestapo while being tortured. On October 20, 1943, she was arrested and confined to Warsaw's notorious Pawiak prison. The Gestapo tortured her in order to find out the names and addresses of the families sheltering the Jewish children. the Nazis broke her body, they could not break her spirit. Irena never betrayed any of her associates or revealed the name of a single child or the family who hid them. Remarkably, she lived to be 98 and died on May 12, 2008.

After three months of intense interrogation, the Gestapo sentenced her to death. However, the Polish underground bribed one of the German officers transporting her to the firing squad. On the execution day, the German officer recorded her name on the list of those already executed. The next day, the Germans loudly proclaimed the news of Irena Sendler's death with posters all over the city. The Gestapo eventually discovered what had really happened and Irena spent the rest of the war in hiding, much like the 2,500 children she had saved. Relentlessly pursued by the Gestapo, she continued her rescue efforts in any way she could. However, 54 days after her escape, ending in March of 1944, the Nazis removed all 500,000 Jews in the Warsaw Ghetto to death camps.

WHY DO SOME ACT AND OTHERS REMAIN SILENT?

STORY 8

Irena Sendler: Life in a Jar

The world can be better,
if there's love, tolerance, and humility.
Irena Sendler

When the war ended, Irena Sendler dug up the jars she had buried beneath the apple tree that contained the names of Jewish children she had rescued. Using the information of the children's true identities and where they had been placed, she began to track down the 2,500 children in hopes of reuniting them with relatives scattered across Europe. Unfortunately, she found that many of their families perished in the Nazi concentration camps such as the Treblinka death camp. Miraculously, she was able to reunite some families and the new nation of Israel welcomed 400 of the children. A few children choose to remain with their adopted Catholic families.

For decades, Irena lived in obscurity in Communist Poland, buried like her jars. In the eyes of the communist government, she was a subversive because of her association with the former Polish government and the underground. Warsaw University refused entry to her son and daughter. At one time, the government sentenced her to death but a Jewish woman official saved her life.

Looking for "Another Schindler"

In 1999, four Protestant high-school girls in rural Kansas uncovered the mostly forgotten story of Irena Sendler. They were completing an assignment for their innovative Social Studies class to report on individuals who made a difference in society. The class motto was: "He who changes one person, changes the entire world." During their research for their National History Day project, the students came across a 1994 *US News and World Report* story entitled *The Other Schindlers*. The article mentioned a Polish Catholic woman named Irena Sendler who had saved 2,500 Jewish children. The teacher thought this was a typographical error because even Schindler had only saved 1,100 Jews. After further research, the students were surprised to learn Irena Sendler was still alive in Poland and that the figures were indeed correct. This discovery dramatically changed their lives and eventually took them to Poland to visit this remarkable woman.

These high-school girls from Kansas introduced Irena Sendler to the world in a short play they wrote with the intriguing title, *Life in a Jar*. The play has been performed hundreds of times and has won numerous awards. From this little play the western news media learned about Irena Sendler and her acts of kindness and courage. The children, whose names were in the jars, had known her only as her code name, Jolanta. As her story became public, she began to receive calls from people who recognized her face from the photos: "I remember your face! You took me out of the ghetto!"

Honors

In a special session in Poland's upper house of Parliament, politicians gathered to honor Mrs. Sendler. One of the children, just six months old when Sendler's resistance group saved her from the ghetto, read a letter from Irena because she was unable to attend. "Every child saved with my help is the justification of my existence on this Earth, and not a title to glory." Israel's ambassador to Poland, David Peleg, said: "She's a great lady, very courageous, and I think she's a model for the whole international community. Her courage is a very special one." Polish President Lech Kaczynski announced the unanimous resolution to honor Mrs. Sendler for rescuing "the most defenseless victims of the Nazi ideology: the Jewish children." He called her a "great heroine who can be justly named for the Nobel Peace Prize. She deserves great respect from our whole nation." Nominated for the Nobel Peace Prize, she finished second to Al Gore's environmental efforts.

Yet, Irena Sendler never saw herself as a heroine. "I only did what was normal. I could have done more," she says. "This regret will follow me to my death." In an interview, she voiced some of her frustrations about how little anything has changed in the world: "After the Second World War it seemed that humanity understood something, and that nothing like that would happen again." "Humanity has understood nothing. Religious, tribal, national wars continue. The world continues to be in a sea of blood."

Characteristically she concluded with a positive word: "The world can be better, if there's love, tolerance, and humility." I would add: and if there are more people with the moral courage and ethical convictions of Irena Sendler to see, hear, feel, speak and act in the face of injustice.

WHY DO SOME ACT AND OTHERS REMAIN SILENT?

STORY 9

Nuremberg Trials: Sins of Commission & Omission

Never forget that everything Hitler did in Germany was legal.
Martin Luther King Jr.
Letter from a Birmingham Jail, April 16, 1963.

Immediately after World War II two sets of courts were formed to bring to justice those guilty of crimes against humanity. The Nuremberg Trials were held from 1945 to 1949 in the German city of Nuremberg at the Nuremberg Palace of Justice.

From November 20, 1945 to October 1, 1946, the International Military Tribunal tried 24 major German Nazi leaders such as Hermann Goring, Rudolf Hess and Albert Speer. These first defendants had set into motion the evil Nazi machine that resulted in the deaths of 60 million in the war, the systematic slaughter of 5 million ethnic undesirables, and the extermination of 6 million Jews. In 1948, an American military tribunal conducted a second set of trials for those charged with lesser crimes such as judges and doctors who served the Nazi regime.

The first trials of the major names were important and certainly more sensational than the second trials. Most of us cannot begin to understand the psychopathic evilness of the true Nazis who were judged and condemned in the first trials. On the other hand, the "lesser" trials provide disturbing lessons for ordinary people who must make moral decisions while living in immoral and even evil circumstances.

Judgment at Nuremberg

The 1961 movie, *Judgment at Nuremberg*, is a dramatized and powerful account of the proceedings at these final trials. Judge Dan Haywood (Spencer Tracy) is the chief judge in the trial of four German judges who are accused of using their offices to authorize Nazi sterilization and racial cleansing policies. One defendant is a senile incompetent, one is an unrepentant Nationalist, one is a good but weak bureaucrat following orders, and one is a respected and strong man caught up in evil. They are accused of knowingly sentencing innocent people to death in collusion with the Nazis.

The character played by Burt Lancaster (Dr. Ernst Janning) was the "strong man caught up in evil." He was basically an honorable man and a good judge who eventually participated in Nazi political judgments from the bench. Lancaster's character was based loosely on a real German judge, Franz Schlegelberger, who was prosecuted for carrying out the injustices of the Nazi government.

Hitler convinced many Germans that the country needed room to grow because it had been unfairly punished fifteen years earlier after their defeat in World War I. The German people for the most part remained silent as Hitler applied his doctrine of *lebensraum* or "living space" and expanded the borders of Germany. One underlying question dominated the trials of these German officials and applied to the German people in general: How much did an ordinary official and German citizen know about the atrocities and injustices?

In the movie, Janning (Lancaster) explained the context of the evil in a passionate statement he made for the trial record over the opposition of his Defense Attorney. "There was a fever on the land of shame and indignity. There was a fear of today, a fear of tomorrow, a fear of our neighbors and a fear of our selves. Hitler said 'lift up your heads. Be proud to be German.'"

"We exceeded beyond our wildest dreams."
"We saw the Rhineland." "Take it!"
"We saw Poland." "Take it!"
"Holland." "Take it!"

"Why did we sit silent and take part? Because we loved our country." "We said that we were only going through a stage and that it would be discarded sooner or later. One day we looked around and what was only to be a passing phase had become a way of life. I was content to sit silent."

"Where were we?" "Where were we when Hitler spewed his hate?" "Where were we when the Jews were taken away? When train terminals were built in every village to carry people to their death? When citizens disappeared and cried out in the night?" "Were we deaf, dumb and blind?"

"Yes! We were aware!" "Maybe we didn't know the details but if we didn't know it was because we didn't want to know. If we were not aware of the extermination of the millions, we were aware of the extermination of the hundreds."

The Defense Lawyer, Hans Rolf (Maximillian Schnell) tried to minimize the damage from Lancaster's emotional confession by asserting corporate guilt. "Ernst Janning's guilt is the world's guilt." This is the classic defense that "everyone is guilty, so no one is guilty."

The message of the movie is brought to a dramatic conclusion in the final scene. The good and strong German judge (Lancaster), who was gradually sucked into the evil, asked the presiding judge (Tracy) to visit him in his jail cell. Tracy stops by the jail as he is going to the airport to return to the United States.

Lancaster first tells Tracy that the harsh sentence is just and he gives Tracy a pre-Nazi edition of his earlier judicial works. As Tracy walks out of the cell, Jannings passionately tries to explain his actions. "Those pictures of the concentration camps." "I never knew it would come to that." "You must believe that."

Tracy stops and sums it all up. "It came to that the first time you wrongly sentenced a man even though you knew he was innocent."

Two Categories of Evil

In the first set of Nuremberg trials, extraordinary evil was being judged. In the second set of trials, ordinary men were being judged. These secondary trials are a disturbing mirror into our ethical souls. They are a reflection of ethical blindness, deafness, insensitivity, hardness of heart and fear. The silence of ordinary and "normal" people transformed them into "willing executioners". The realization that ordinary people can look the other way or even condone or participate in injustice pushes our comfort level where we don't want to go. In the second set of trials, tribunal judges often found themselves confronting the ethical question of how much responsibility someone held who had "just followed orders." Is guilt attached to silence?

These two levels of trials show how evil and ethics break down into two distinct categories. Evil can be a commission of intention and evil can be an omission of action. An act of commission is active and willful. On the other hand, an act of omission is passive and appears to be guiltless. Commission is what I do and omission is what I fail to do or prevent from being done.

These subtle distinctions in ethical behavior reach all the way down into the lives of ordinary people and situations in every period of history. Overt acts of commission eventually expose themselves as good or evil. However, acts of omission that are cloaked in fear, indifference and silence are more difficult to expose and to categorize as just or unjust.

It is important to understand that omission is not a benign neutral state but, like silence, omission is a choice. Those who commit the sin of omission decide to be indifferent. They refuse to make a difference when they can make a difference.

It complicates our simplistic understanding of ethics to realize that God attaches a level of guilt to acts of omission.

WHY DO SOME ACT AND OTHERS REMAIN SILENT?

STORY 10

Nickolas Winton: The Last Train

Save one life, save the world.
The Jewish Talmud

Nicholas Winton, a 29-year-old London stockbroker, was packing to go skiing in Switzerland just before Christmas of 1938. He was interrupted by an urgent phone call from a friend in Czechoslovakia. "I need your help in Prague." "Cancel your holiday." "By the way, don't bring your skis."

When Winton arrived in Czechoslovakia, he was asked to help relieve the suffering of hundreds of Jews who were living in appalling conditions.

This human crisis was caused by several events playing out on the stage of history during the last months of 1938. The events were all connected to the evil mind of Adolph Hitler. The ill-fated Munich Agreement between Germany and the Western European powers began the terrible process that led to the Holocaust and World War II. Representatives from Germany, France, Britain, and Italy met in Munich to discuss the territorial demands of Hitler. The dictator declared his intention to annex the Sudetenland, a region of Czechoslovakia populated largely by ethnic Germans. Britain and France, who had adopted a policy of appeasement toward Hitler, pressured Czechoslovakia to give in to Hitler's totally illegal demands. The agreement to give Hitler the Sudetenland was signed on September 30, 1938 but dated September 29. No Czech representative was present at the conference or signed the agreement that led to the destruction of the Czech state.

Winston Churchill understood the Munich Agreement would not appease Hitler. "Do not suppose that this is the end. This is only the beginning of the reckoning."

The Night of Broken Glass

Six weeks after the Munich Agreement, the Nazis began violent attacks against German and Austrian Jews on the nights of November 9 and 10, 1938. The event was called "Kristallnacht" which means the "night of broken glass." The name came from the shattered windowpanes of the Jewish shops, businesses, department stores, and homes destroyed that night. Nazi propaganda called it a "spontaneous outburst of public sentiment" in response to the assassination of German diplomat Ernst vom Rath by a 17-year-old German-born Polish Jew.

Thousands of Jewish homes and businesses along with 267 synagogues were destroyed and ransacked by the SS, SA storm troopers, the Gestapo, the Hitler Youth, and ordinary Germans caught up in the mass hysteria. The soldiers rounded up 30,000 Jewish men and sent to Buchenwald, Dachau, and Sacksenhausen where hundreds died within weeks of arrival. Release came after three months for those who agreed to leave Germany and to transfer their property to "pure" Germans.

Historian Max Rein concluded in 1988: "Kristallnacht came . . . and everything was changed." The nature of the Nazis' persecution changed from economic, political, and social pressure to physical beatings, incarceration, and murder. Most see this night as the beginning of the Holocaust.

Hermann Goring first publicly discussed the Jewish "final solution" in a speech on the night after Kristallnacht. The head of Germany's Air Force and heir apparent to Hitler explained what would happen. "The Jewish problem will reach its solution if, in any time soon, we will be drawn into war beyond our borders . . . then it is obvious that we will have to manage a final account with the Jews."

The historical events of the Munich Agreement, the Night of Broken Glass, and the expulsion of Jews from Germany set into motion a counter-action to save the Jewish children of Europe from Hitler before it was too late.

The Last Transport

Alarmed by Hitler's threats and actions against Jews, Jewish and Christian agencies began rescuing German and Austrian Jewish children on *Kindertransporten* (children's transports). Between December 1938 and May 1939, almost 10,000 children (infants to teenagers) were rescued and given shelter at farms, hostels, camps, and in private homes in Britain. However, this effort did not include the children of Czechoslovakia.

After Nicholas Winton saw the situation at the refugee camp, he set up his own rescue operation for the children in Czechoslovakia. Over a period of nine months in 1939, Winton organized eight rescue trains that took 669 children from the Wilson Railway Station in Prague, Czechoslovakia by train, boat and finally by train again to the Liverpool Train Station in London. He helped raise the required money (£50 for each child) and completed the extensive legal paperwork to place the children in the hands of foster families.

In an interview in September of 2009 at the age of 100, he talked about meeting each of the eight trains at the Liverpool Train Station and the hectic procedure of placing the proper child with the family that was receiving them.

In the same interview, Winton shared that his most painful memory was the last transport that did not get out. "Of all the transports the one that didn't succeed affects me the most." On September 1, 1939, the very day Hitler invaded Poland, 250 children boarded a ninth train in Prague. 250 foster families awaited them at London's Liverpool Street station. However, the war began and the children were never allowed to leave.

Winton stated that only one or two of the children on the last transport lived. "In the main they perished." Most of the 15,000 Jewish children remaining in Czechoslovakia died during the next six years of war.

Passive and Active Goodness

An excerpt from a letter Winton wrote in May of 1939 explains the thinking of those who accepted the task of rescuing the children. "There is a difference between passive goodness and active goodness, which is, in my opinion, the giving of one's time and energy in the alleviation of pain and suffering. It entails going out, finding and helping those in suffering and danger, and not merely in leading an exemplary life, in a purely passive way of doing no wrong."

Active goodness is a recurring theme in Winton's life. In 2008, a young woman asked him "If you could give one piece of advice for future generations, something you have learned from your life, what would it be?" After a long contemplative pause, he paraphrased the theme of his life. "Don't be content in your life just to do no wrong, be prepared every day to try to do something good."

Winton was asked in an interview about the impact on his life of his experience with the children. "Whether by luck or good management it has been the greatest thing that I have done." "I don't allot to it the fame I am getting. It seemed to me something quite natural to do."

He still wears a ring given him by some of the children he saved. It is inscribed with a line from the Talmud, the book of Jewish law. "Save one life, save the world."

STORY 11

Corrie ten Boom: Deep Pits

There is no pit so deep the love of God is not deeper still.
Corrie ten Boom

In the early days of the German occupation of Holland, Corrie ten Boom asked a pastor who was visiting their home to help shield a mother and newborn infant from the Nazis. The pastor replied, "No definitely not! We could lose our lives for that Jewish child."

Corrie went on, "Unseen by either of us, Father had appeared in the doorway. 'Give the child to me, Corrie,' he said. Father held the baby close, his white beard brushing its cheek, looking into the little face with eyes as blue and innocent as the baby's. 'You say we could lose our lives for this child. I would consider that the greatest honor that could come to my family.'"

This statement by Caspar ten Boom helps us understand the character and courage of his family in the face of great tribulation and injustice.

Christian Resistance

When German forces invaded Holland on May 10, 1940 the ten Boom family began to help the Jews with small acts of kindness. Eventually the entire family became part of the underground resistance that protected Jews. Willem, the oldest child and a pastor, lived on the outskirts of the city where his home became a staging area for the resistance movement and a transit center for moving Jews out of the country.

Caspar, Betsie and Corrie built a special hiding place for Jews in their home in Haarlem and were able to operate underground undetected for 3 ½ years during the German occupation.

A man Corrie was trying to help betrayed them to the Gestapo. Consequently, the entire ten Boom family was arrested on February 28, 1944 for possessing illegal ration-cards used to feed Jews. The Gestapo never did locate the hiding place or its last occupants.

Four members of the ten Boom family would lose their lives in less than two years from the time of their arrest. Caspar ten Boom died at the age of 84 after only ten days in Scheveningen Prison. Betsie died in the Ravensbruck concentration camp a few days before Christmas 1944 at the age of 59. Their brother, Willem contracted spinal tuberculosis while in prison and died at the age of 60 about the same time as Betsie. Willem's son Kik was sent to Bergen Belsen for his part in the resistance and died as a German prisoner of war.

Ravensbruck

Betsie and Corrie were shipped to Ravensbruck in Northern Germany after their arrest and brief stays in two prisons in Holland. 35,000 female prisoners at one time were crowded into this infamous work camp for women near Berlin. The conditions were deplorable, humiliating and deadly. 130,000 female prisoners passed through the system at Ravensbruck and only 40,000 survived.

This means that when three women entered Ravensbruck, only one would eventually leave alive. At their ages, for Betsie and Corrie Ravensbruck was a death sentence.

Later Corrie explained what sustained her during those terrible days. "When I was a little girl I went to my father and said, "Daddy, I am afraid that I will never be strong enough to be a martyr for Jesus Christ." "Tell me," said Father, "When you take a train trip to Amsterdam, when do I give you the money for the ticket? Three weeks before?" "No, Daddy, you give me the money for the ticket just before we get on the train."

"That is right," my father said, "and so it is with God's strength. Our Father in Heaven knows when you will need the strength to be a martyr for Jesus Christ. He will supply all you need . . . just in time . . ."

The Crazy Place, Where They Hope

Barracks 28 was built to accommodate 400 people but Betsie and Corrie were packed together with 1400 other prisoners. The survivors described life there as "hell on earth." However, even in Ravensbruck Betsie and Corrie continued to minister and encourage. They held clandestine Bible studies under a single light bulb using the Bible that Corrie had smuggled past the prison guards.

In a radio interview Corrie explained why they could have a Bible study under the noses of the Nazi guards. "The guards would only enter the barracks in a time of extreme emergency because of the disease, fleas and lice." Corrie laughed that the fleas and lice were a blessing from God.

Corrie describes the meetings: "These were services like no others, these times in Barracks 28. A single meeting night might include a recital of *The Magnificant* in Latin by a group of Roman Catholics, a whispered hymn by some Lutherans, and a sotto-voce chant by Eastern Orthodox women. With each moment the crowd around us would swell, packing nearby platforms, hanging over the edges, until the high structures groaned and swayed."

"At last either Betsie or I would open the Bible. Because only the Hollanders could understand the Dutch text we would translate aloud in German. And then we would hear the life-giving words passed back along the aisles in French, Polish, Russian, Czech, and back into Dutch. They were little previews of heaven, these evenings beneath the light bulb." (*The Hiding Place*; Ten Boom 1971, p. 201.)

Corrie explained: "To the other prisoners Barracks 28 became known as 'the crazy place, where they hope.'" Even in this evil place Corrie "let God's promises shine on her problems."

The Special Word from God

In the unlikely place of Ravensbruck both Betsie and Corrie learned an important truth about God. Corrie remembers that between the two of them Betsie had the most faith and hope in this truth. However, Corrie would be the one to share that truth around the world.

Just before she died, Betsie restated their special truth to Corrie. "When we are set free from this terrible place . . . and we will be freed, Corrie, before the new year . . . we must go over the world and tell everyone who will listen to what we have proved to be true in this terrible place: that the love of God is stronger than the deepest darkness. They will believe us because we were here."

Before the end of the year, Betsie was set free in death and Corrie by a "clerical error" on Christmas Day of 1944. Corrie later learned that the week after her release all women her age at Ravensbruck were executed.

For thirty-three years after their time in Ravensbruck, and in more than 60 countries, Corrie shared their truth for Betsie in one of her most powerful quotes. "There is no pit so deep the love of God is not deeper still."

STORY 12

Corrie ten Boom: The Ethics of Forgiveness

Forgiveness is an act of the will, and the will can function regardless of the temperature of the heart.
Corrie ten Boom

In the dreadful conditions in Ravensbruck, Corrie ten Boom found herself struggling with hatred toward the man who had betrayed her family. She was inspired by Betsie's example of selfless love and forgiveness in the midst of the inhuman indignity, extreme cruelty and brutal persecution. However, Corrie continued to harbor bitter unforgiveness in her heart for those who were abusing them, especially fragile Betsie.

One of Corrie's most powerful experiences took place in the third year after Betsie's death and her release from Ravensbruck concentration camp. While on a trip to Germany, she came face to face with "one of the cruelest former camp guards." This encounter forced her to deal with her feelings and with forgiveness. She shares the account in her autobiography *The Hiding Place*. This incident is reprinted in *Guideposts*.

Nazi Prison Guard

"It was in a church in Munich that I saw him, a balding heavy-set man in a gray overcoat, a brown felt hat clutched between his hands. People were filing out of the basement room where I had just spoken. It was 1947 and I had come from Holland to defeated Germany with the message that God forgives.

"And that's when I saw him, working his way forward against the others. One moment I saw the overcoat and the brown hat; the next, a blue uniform and a visored cap with its skull and crossbones.

It came back with a rush: the huge room with its harsh overhead lights, the pathetic pile of dresses and shoes in the center of the floor, the shame of walking naked past this man. I could see my sister's frail form ahead of me, ribs sharp beneath the parchment skin. Betsie, how thin you were!

"Betsie and I had been arrested for concealing Jews in our home during the Nazi occupation of Holland; this man had been a guard at Ravensbruck concentration camp where we were sent.

'You mentioned Ravensbruck in your talk, he was saying. 'I was a guard in there. No, he did not remember me.

'But since that time,' he went on, 'I have become a Christian. I know that God has forgiven me for the cruel things I did there, but I would like to hear it from your lips as well. Fraulein, ...' his hand came out, . . . 'will you forgive me?

"And I stood there . . . I whose sins had every day to be forgiven . . . and could not. Betsie had died in that place . . . could he erase her slow terrible death simply for the asking?

It could not have been many seconds that he stood there, hand held out, but to me it seemed hours as I wrestled with the most difficult thing I had ever had to do.

"For I had to do it . . . I knew that. The message that God forgives has a prior condition: that we forgive those who have injured us. 'If you do not forgive men their trespasses,' Jesus says, 'neither will your Father in heaven forgive your trespasses.' . . ."

You Supply the Feeling

"And still I stood there with the coldness clutching my heart. But forgiveness is not an emotion . . . I knew that too. Forgiveness is an act of the will, and the will can function regardless of the temperature of the heart. 'Jesus, help me!' I prayed silently. 'I can lift my hand, I can do that much. You supply the feeling.'

"And so woodenly, mechanically, I thrust my hand into the one stretched out to me. And as I did, an incredible thing took place. The current started in my shoulder, raced down my arm, sprang into our joined hands. And then this healing warmth seemed to flood my whole being, bringing tears to my eyes. 'I forgive you, brother!' I cried. 'With all my heart!'

For a long moment we grasped each other's hands, the former guard and the former prisoner. I had never known God's love so intensely as I did then."
(*Guideposts*, Copyright; 1972 by Guideposts, Carmel. New York 10512.)

For the rest of her life as a speaker and storyteller, Corrie looked back at this experience as the one moment she most felt the love of God surging through her.

HISTORICAL & PERSONAL STORIES FROM SLAVERY & SEGREGATION

WE ALL HAVE AN ETHICAL STORY!

"There is a history in all men's lives."
Shakespeare

EXPLANATION

The term used to designate a race of people is always sensitive. To complicate matters, these terms have a historical context and change from generation to generation. The term used at one point in history may not be acceptable in a later period of history. Some terms may even come back into use after earlier rejection. In addition, different terms for race may be used in different countries and regions within countries. The fact that we use technical and common terms also adds to the confusion. We use some terms in writing and others in speaking. We use some terms in private and some in public. In addition, groups use some terms to refer to themselves that they reject when used by those outside of their group. Society also has its own formal set of terms for groups. Then we have the derogatory terms that are used to hurt and demean. Some terms that started off innocently become ethnic slurs because of usage.

Therefore, I ask for your indulgence and forgiveness as I try to use the proper terms for race in the following stories. I have chosen to use the terminology of the period in which the story is set. Because the terms were evolving, several terms may be mixed together in the same story or conversation. I have chosen to use names for Black Americans that were the most respectful within the context of segregation. When possible, I have chosen terms Black Americans used.

At the time of these stories, Black Americans were referred to as "Coloreds," "Negroes," and "Blacks" and African Americans. In fact, at a certain point some Black Americans demanded to be called "Blacks" instead of "Negroes." Dr. King and other Civil Rights leaders used all of these terms during the course of the Civil Rights Movement. I avoid using the derogatory names that were also used during the time periods of the different stories.

The term used by both European and Black Americans for European Americans was "whites." In this paper, I have chosen to capitalize "Black" and not capitalize "white". However, when a term is period-sensitive I use the form of the time.

WHY DO SOME ACT AND OTHERS REMAIN SILENT?

STORY 13

The "Will" of God

I have a dream that my four little children
will one day live in a nation where they
will not be judged by the color of their
skin, but by the content of their character.
Martin Luther King Jr.
August 28, 1963

The 1950 movie, *Stars in My Crown,* is probably considered a minor movie in Hollywood, but it is one of my favorites. It is adapted from a novel by Joe David Brown. Some theorize that this rather obscure novel influenced Harper Lee when she wrote her classic and only work, *To Kill a Mockingbird.*

The events take place after the Civil War in the small town of Walesburg somewhere in the South. In the movie, Joel McCrea plays Parson Grey, a Civil War veteran and gospel minister. As the spiritual presence of God, he combats the sinister influence of the Night Riders (Ku Klux Klan). The events are seen and told through the eyes and memory of John, the parson's young grandson who is part of his family. (In the book John is a more distant relative). Walesburg reminds me of both the simplicity of life and the complexity of social relationships in my hometown.

Juano Hernandez plays Uncle Famous Phrill, the former slave who was a friend to most of the men in the town when they were boys. A vein of mica ore is located on Uncle Famous' small piece of property and the ore vein is running out in the local mine that is a primary source of employment in the town. Lon Hamilton, the owner of the local mine, needs the ore. He offers to buy Uncle Famous' house and land for $16.00. Uncle Famous doesn't want to sell his property and the mine owner sets about to force him to sell by using the Night Riders. Even though he is threatened, Uncle Famous won't sell, and now the Night Riders plan to lynch him.

Parson Grey and his grandson, who is hiding under the porch, are with Uncle Famous in the middle of the night when the mob comes for him at his little cabin. The boy tells the story in his own words and dialect.

The Will

The moon shone on their white sheets. They didn't seem to have heads . . . just two black holes for their eyes. They seemed to be from another world. I was scared . . . so scared that my hands were cold. I could feel my heart beating in my throat.

When they were about twenty yards from the cabin, they stopped. The four white figures in front lighted pine torches. Then, without a word, they moved forward again. Two of the Night Riders grabbed Uncle Famous and another put a rope around his neck. The rope had been ready all the time. It was big and thick and had a long ugly knot in it.

They started to hustle Uncle Famous off of the porch when Grandpa spoke. "I was asked by Uncle Famous to help set everything right. We've prayed together and we've talked together. Uncle Famous has even made a will and I have it here." Grandpa reached into his big side pocket and pulled out a sheaf of papers. He slapped the papers against his other hand. "Here's the will, and it's all legal and witnessed."

You could see that set that crowd up right smart. There was just one thing on everybody's mind. Just who was going to get that farm and its mica vein? They all knew Uncle Famous didn't have much else.

Grandpa cleared his throat sort of legal-like. "Now, men, just so there can't be any arguments about this, I'd like to read this will right here in front of Uncle Famous so you can see it's legal. After you all hear it, and know that it's really his, you can go about your work." Half a dozen voices spoke out consent to this.

Grandpa nodded a little thank you, cleared his throat and stepped back into the circle of light from the cabin door. As an afterthought, he stopped. "I took this will down in Uncle Famous' own words. It isn't in lawyer form, but just as he spoke it. I hope you understand that." Then, he began Uncle Famous' will:

"I ain't been able to lay much by in my life, but the things I have, I want to go to my friends. I got forty dollars in the Farmers and Merchants Bank and I want to leave it to Mister Earnest Caldwell. The day he was born, his daddy took me to see him, all wrinkled and red. I wanted to give him something then, but I didn't have nothing. I hopes he takes the forty dollars, even if it is thirty years late. My fishing poles I leave to Mister Clem Shelton. I teached him to catch sun perch when he was a little boy. He never had much luck. I told him it was because I had a magic pole. His eyes use to shine at that. Maybe now he can catch some fish.

"My rusty old steel traps I leaves to Mister Rufus Belsher. They ain't much good, but when Mister Belsher was about eight he use to say he was going to the North Woods and be a trapper. Maybe now he can learn his littlest boy to catch muskrats. I sure wants Mister Perry Lokey to have my watermelon patch. He was a full-grown man before he quit snitching my melons, and he knowed I seen him, too.

"That double-barreled old shotgun of mine, I leaves to Mister Lem Parsons. When he was a little boy he shot it off at a cottontail, and it knocked him plumb over a rail fence. He's big enough and man enough to handle it now."

There wasn't a sound in that crowd as Grandpa read. It was just still and quiet, and then I noticed a strange thing. Grandpa was reading, but nobody was looking at him. Every eye was on Uncle Famous. And it was Uncle Famous' voice they heard, just the way he talked, even though his lips weren't moving.

His will rolled on. "My hogs I leaves to Mister Thad Hankins. How that boy did love barbeque! Weren't hardly possible to cook it without him coming around. I hopes he has a big barbeque and invites all our friends. My tools I give to Mister John Gailbraith. He always liked to help me sharpen my axe, and I reckon now he is the best sawmill boss in the world."

Uncle Famous didn't forget many people in that will of his, and as he parceled out his few possessions, he had a little story to tell about every man. Bill Hicks got his razor. Taylor Mackay got his trotlines. Justin Beggs got his chickens and there were just lots more.

Finally Grandpa came to the last page. He read very slow now and his voice was heavy and melodious. "I want all the mica glass on my property to go to Mister Lon Hamilton. Mister Hamilton wants that glass powerful bad, and now he can have it. I leaves him all he can find on my farm. I always found it a bother myself. There is something else I wants to leave Mister Hamilton. I wants him to have my Bible. It ain't fancy I guess. It's almost worn out, but I wants Mister Hamilton to have it. I hopes he reads it."

That was all. That was the will of Famous Phrill. Grandpa stopped reading and just stood there. Nobody made a sound. Nobody moved. Grandpa spoke real low: "You can have him now, men." Somehow it sounded like a benediction. The pine torches had flickered out, and all the noises of the night closed about us. Then one man moved. He stepped up to Uncle Famous and took the rope from his neck. He threw it down like it was dirty and then turned and headed straight back through that crowd. It made way for him, and then gradually, it began to dissolve. There wasn't a word spoken. The men just went away slowly and quietly.

Big tears were running down Uncle Famous' old face. He turned and shook Grandpa's hand. "Thank you, Parson." Then he laid a hand on my head and went into the cabin. Grandpa reached for his handkerchief, and when he did Uncle Famous' will fell to the floor. I reached to pick it up. As my hands reached the white pages, I gasped. The pages were blank. Just four pieces of white, unmarked paper.

"Grandpa," I began, "this isn't a wi . . .!" Grandpa looked down quickly. He took the papers, and stuffed them into his big pocket. Then he smiled sort of calm-like. "Yes it is, son. It's the will of God."

Then he took my little paw into his big hand and we walked into the night while the katydids sang around us.

The Village Church

The conclusion of the story is both poignant and prophetic. The scene is inside the village church on Sunday morning. Parson Grey sits at the front of the auditorium facing the congregation. The parson's wife is playing the pump organ and John is pumping away. The characters in the story are in the pews, including Lon Hamilton the leader of the Night Riders. We also see the cynical young doctor who found faith after the parson successfully prayed for his fiancé who was near death.

The church doors begin to close by an invisible hand and frame Uncle Famous in the distance. He walks along the road in his overalls with his fishing pole as the four little puppies of his hunting dog Belle bounce along around him.

The door closes after the wife and five sons of Jed, the town's unbeliever and the Parson's special friend from the War, make their entrance into the building. Finally, Jed, the loveable reprobate, opens the door, hesitantly sticks his head in and finally walks into the auditorium. The Parson's wife begins to play the Parson's favorite hymn "Will There be any Stars in My Crown." The Parson walks down and warmly welcomes Jed.

Everyone is in the fold of the church . . . except Uncle Famous. He is still outside. Nearly another century will pass before the social and religious prejudice in the South is exposed and broken so Uncle Famous is also welcome inside the church. The last stories in this book are about some of my experiences and special friends in the towns and churches of my youth as the doors finally opened to people like Uncle Famous.

WHY DO SOME ACT AND OTHERS REMAIN SILENT?

STORY 14

Connections to the Past

*It is true that behavior cannot be legislated,
and legislation cannot make you love me, but
legislation can restrain you from lynching me,
and I think that is kind of important.*
Martin Luther King, Jr.
November 13, 1962

During our thirty-minute lunch break, my Father's crew of bricklayers was discussing the unusual topic of "lynching." In the course of the conversation, my Father shared a boyhood experience that shocked me.

His story took place in my father's hometown where my grandfather lived until his death at the age of 97. As my father told his story, I could visualize the place he was describing because I had been there many times. The courthouse stands in the center of the "second largest square in Texas" and businesses face the courthouse on the four streets. Cars park in the marked spaces between the courthouse and the businesses. Large oak, elm and pecan trees shade the common lawn area surrounding the courthouse. The north-south and east-west roads passing through the town center are slowed to a crawl around the square by stop signs at the four intersections. All life stops at the town square.

While walking through the town square, my father came upon a large mob of men that had broken into the jail and was in the process of lynching a young Black man. I asked my father,

"What did he do?" "He was accused of killing a white woman." Some boys my father knew yelled out to him: "Jimmie, help us with this rope." My father said he continued walking away and "didn't want to have anything to do with what was happening."

The Picture

Research verifies my father's story and adds disturbing details to the event. Newspapers report that on August 2, 1920, at Center, Texas, Lige Daniels, a young Black man, was forcibly removed from jail and lynched in the town square. He was only a few years older than my 13- year-old Father, who hurried past the mob scene.

Today these kinds of scenes are captured only on black and white photographs in museums, libraries and movies. However, in 1920 in Texas this picture was put on a postcard that was widely sold as a souvenir and collectors-item. The black and white photo shows the gruesome scene with the body hanging from a large oak tree over the heads of the mob. The courthouse, the place of promised justice, is the backdrop for this obscene act of injustice. The crowd stands beneath the tree as if posing for a picture for a town picnic.

Four boys, one about the age of my father and the others slightly younger, stand at the front of the picture. The oldest boy is looking up slightly and has a grin on his face that is obscenely out of place. These are the only boys in the crowd and therefore may very well be the ones who called out to my father. It is difficult for me to imagine his feelings as he carried this scene around in his mind. I wonder what caused him to walk away rather than to join the other boys in the lynch mob. I feel great relief that he is not in the picture.

There were no hooded men in white sheets in the picture of the surprisingly well-dressed crowd of men in the picture.

However, almost certainly the Ku Klux Klan, or something like it, was behind the lynching on that hot August afternoon in 1920. The Ku Klux Klan instigated or carried out the lynching of hundreds of Blacks along with acts of violence and intimidations in order to maintain segregation.

It is frightening to realize that those committing this lawless act on that day in 1920 did not feel they needed the cover of night or hoods to cover their faces. This lynching was sanctioned in broad daylight by the community.

Conversation in a Peach Orchard

Fifty years after the lynching, I was helping my father in his retirement peach orchard during my vacation. A peach orchard of a thousand trees demands a lot of labor during picking season. Some of my father's retired friends helped him, more for the camaraderie and free peaches than for the minimum wages. His work force included my old high school principal, my mother and aunt who were public school teachers, and several local retired businessmen. Counting my father, four of the workers that year were Baptist deacons, and one of those was one of my Sunday School teachers when I was a boy. Among the group was a 75-year-old retired grocer. As a boy I grew up knowing him as a deacon, a community leader and a personal friend of my family. When my father was in the Pacific Theatre during World War II, my mother never had to worry about a bill at his grocery store. He was a genuine friend and would say, "Don't worry Julia. Pay when you can."

We were discussing a racial incident in a nearby town and the subject of the Ku Klux Klan came up. Mr. Otto casually mentioned that he had been a member of the Ku Klux Klan decades before in an adjoining State. This did not surprise me because I knew the Klan had been active in that part of the country.

What shocked me was his added casual comment that the Klan "did a lot of good." He gave examples of the Klan visiting a man who was not properly caring for his family or warning a man who was "running around on his wife." In his interpretation of history, the Klan was regulating behavior in a segment of life that the law could not touch. He made the Klan sound like a righteous fraternal organization.

I was deeply disturbed that this ethical and social evil could exist within this "good" person and that social evil could be explained in "good" terms.

Connections

My family connections remind me of the nearness of ethical evil. I am linked to slavery through my ancestors, to the Ku Klux Klan through the experience of my father, and to segregation through my own personal experience. I am only one generation removed from a lynching, only three generations removed from institutional slavery and I lived through segregation.

Historical connections give perspective through which we learn the lessons of the past and apply them to the present. These stories about slavery and segregation connect the dots for my grandchildren through me to ethical and unethical events and the mingling of the two.

It is important to remember these links to our past because "he who ignores history is doomed to repeat it." History, properly applied, can give light to the dark and crooked path through this broken and fallen world.

STORY 15

Front-street & Back-street

*The line separating good and evil passes not through
states, nor between classes, nor between political
parties either . . . but through all human hearts.*
Aleksandr I. Solzhenitsyn
Gulag Archipelago

My hometown was divided between front-street and back-street. The real names of the streets were Quitman Street and Fulton Street but we called them "Front Street" and "Back Street." The names were more than a geographical location. Front-street and back-street was a state of mind and a fact of life that cut through all of society within the city limits, passing through the restaurants, movie theater, drinking fountains, public toilets, churches, and even cemeteries.

I did not realize it at the time but in 1939 I was born into the middle of a great social, political, economic and religious battle about basic human rights and ethics. I was part of the final battle of the Civil War that had turned into a one-hundred-year engagement called "segregation." The battle line for that engagement ran through the front-street and back-street of my hometown and through the hearts and social awareness of every citizen.

An Early Memory

In one of my early childhood memories, I am sitting with my brother in our black 1941 Chevy Sedan on the Southside of

Front-street on a beautiful Saturday afternoon. The time is after World War II but before we bought our 1947 brown and tan Chevy. We are parked in front of Otto's Grocery Store and our parents are shopping and visiting.

The sidewalks are crowded because everyone "went to town" on Saturday afternoon. The dress is not Sunday best but special, and all the men wear hats of some description. Every parking space is filled on the north and south sides of Main Street. People are going in and out of the stores, greeting each other and talking in small groups in the shade of the awning that extends from the storefronts over the sidewalk to the two-foot-high curb.

Upon closer inspection of that early memory, everyone on front-street is white. I don't see one Black person even though more than 30% of the population is Black. Certainly, I do not see any Black people going in the front entrances of the stores. The white people did business and interacted socially on front-street while the Black people carried out their business and social activities on back-street.

Perry Brothers Five & Dime Store, in the center of town at the southeast corner of the red light, had separate drinking fountains for Whites and Blacks. All public toilets at the Court House and gas stations were labeled "For Whites Only" or "For Coloreds Only." The restaurants on front-street were restricted "For Whites Only." At the local movie theater, an outside door and stairway led Blacks to their seats in the balcony. The churches on front-street did not have a "For Whites Only" sign posted at the door, but everyone observed the invisible signs.

Front-street and back-street even extended into the cemeteries. Rosehill Cemetery, located on a hill at the eastern edge of town, had a special "colored" section in the bottom part of the Cemetery. A barbed wire fence separated the tombstones in

Cedar Grove Cemetery where Black people were buried from the tombstones in Rose Hill Cemetery where white people were buried. This invisible line for the dead passed through all of the smaller church and private cemeteries throughout the country.

The invisible line also stretched beyond the business district. Whites had their own neighborhoods and sub-divisions and Blacks had their designated sections of town, mostly "across the tracks." For those who lived outside of the city limits in the County, the lines were not as rigid. Blacks and whites might live adjacent to each other on farms and individual houses if a proper distance or a barrier of trees or a pasture were between. However, the basic front-street and back-street social rules still applied.

Children of the South

No one explained to the children in my hometown about the front-street and back-street demarcation line that governed the interaction of the races. I never remember a sermon, school lesson or civic speech that defended or denounced the segregated system in my hometown. I learned the rules of the front-street and back-street arrangement from observation and from remarks in daily conversation that clearly put every person "in their place."

The song from the musical *South Pacific* explains what was happening in cities, towns, and villages across the south. "Children must be carefully taught to hate." White children were gradually introduced to this terrible attitude of hate with more subtle terms. Unfortunately, the end result was the same: Prejudice and hate.

White children learned the rules early and easily because of the benefits of being the privileged class in the system. Voices of government, family, and even church told us that separating people by the color of their skin was normal and acceptable. The front-street and back-street arrangement was so "normal" we didn't even see it. White children also learned about front-street and back-street from each other. Unfortunately, that was often a distorted and cruel version of their parent's view.

I can only imagine the pain of the learning process for the Black children. Black children had to be carefully taught to be hated, to be demeaned, and to "know their place" on back-street. It was dangerous, even a matter of life and death, if a Black child did not learn their place. Remember the lynching story.

How do parents teach a child to be on the receiving end of Prejudice? How is a bright, beautiful baby with the God-given sense of inherent worth prepared to accept inequality?

I cringe when I think of that moment when a Black child first understood that he or she would be the object of prejudice, hate and inequality, and must passively accept it. Imagine that moment when a child found out that value and worth depended on skin color. That may be the most horrible moment of slavery and segregation.

Yes, the violent physical acts of prejudice and hate are unthinkable. However, when prejudice and hate was forced into the consciousness of a Black child, that was violence against the spirit and soul, and violence against the God who created that child.

Parallel Worlds

Rosa Parks recalls as a young child watching buses take white students to their new school while Black students walked to theirs. "I'd see the bus pass every day . . . but to me, that was a way of life; we had no choice but to accept what was the custom. The bus was among the first ways I realized there was a Black world and a white world."

The concept of parallel worlds, one privileged and one second-class, does irreparable damage to the souls of the child chosen for the privileged world and the child condemned to the second-class world.

In a letter written from the Birmingham jail to a group of white clergymen, Martin Luther King, Jr. speaks about segregation from the perspective of a parent trying to explain segregation to a child.

"You suddenly find your tongue twisted and your speech stammering as you seek to explain to your six year old daughter why she can't go to the public amusement park that has just been advertised on television, and see tears welling up in her eyes when she is told that Funtown is closed to colored children, and see ominous clouds of inferiority beginning to form in her little mental sky, and see her beginning to distort her personality by developing an unconscious bitterness toward white people."

"You have to concoct an answer for a five-year-old son who is asking: 'Daddy, why do white people treat colored people so mean?'"

WHY DO SOME ACT AND OTHERS REMAIN SILENT?

STORY 16

Hot Links & Social Change

*In the end, we will remember not the words of our enemies,
but the silence of our friends.*
Martin Luther King
March 8, 1965, the day after "Bloody Sunday".

The eating arrangements in my hometown were carefully controlled. This was necessary because eating together is one of the highest forms of social acceptance and recognition. Joining around a meal establishes a certain common bond of equal need and rights. It is the first step toward "life, liberty and the pursuit of happiness." Jesus taught us to pray, "Give us *our* daily bread." Sharing a meal with someone suggests equality and humanity and therefore opens the dangerous possibility of other social contacts in business, church, the voting booth, and school. Controlling the eating arrangements was necessary for maintaining a culture that separated the races. This explains the "For Whites Only" signs in the front windows of restaurants.

The hands of Black cooks prepared much of the food that was consumed in public restaurants and in many homes. Yet they were not allowed to sit at the table with whites and eat the food they prepared. In certain situations, coloreds could receive a meal in the back of a white restaurant. Food prepared in homes was eaten first by the family and then by the cooks. The "help" didn't eat with the family. This may have had an employer and employee component but it was also racial because the "help" was almost always colored.

Hot Links

Sometime around 1900, a German immigrant began selling a tasty sausage in my hometown that was a little larger than a man's thumb after it was cooked. The sausages were linked together with the covering in which the meat was stuffed, slow-cooked, and served hot. So the tasty treat was called "Hot Links." The local delicacy dripped with grease, was made with unpublished ingredients, was totally dangerous to one's health, but was sinfully delicious. Locals raised on hot links know they are extremely addictive.

Otto's Grocery Store and Mr. King's Busy Bee Market sold hot links in the back of their grocery stores. Eventually Mr. James had a place that just sold hot links. Entrance for whites was gained directly from the back-street or through the store that opened to the front-street. Blacks always used the back-street entrance. Since Busy Bee Market and James' Hot Links were already on back-street, Blacks usually entered the back entrance of back-street.

A Hot Link Joint did not have tables and chairs but counters and benches that were arranged in a square or rectangle. Inside the square was everything necessary to serve the hot links: the stove, cash register, cold drink box, cashier, waitresses, crackers, hot sauce and butcher paper that served as plates.

I can still smell the links and feel the dark cool atmosphere of the Hot Link Joint. My usual order would be six hot links, all the saltine crackers I could eat, and a Double Cola, a local soft drink. I paid 25 cents for the links and 5 cents for the drink.

Not only was a Hot Link Joint a unique eating experience, it was also a unique social experience. For some inexplicable reason, the rules of front-street and back-street were suspended inside a Hot Link Joint where the seating arrangement broke the normal rules of social etiquette. Whites and Blacks actually ate together facing each other.

However, there was an "invisible" line even in the Hot Link Joint. The white people ate on one side and the Black's sat on the other side. Conversation was restricted to polite greetings across the invisible barrier between the two sections. But whites and Blacks did eat the same food, in the same room, at the same time, and for the same price.

In addition to the Hot Link Joint, some informal meals were exempt from the eating protocols. My Father's workforce ate their sack lunches together at noon under the same shade. Time seemed to stand still as it ticked down to 12 o'clock. If we were out hunting, chasing cows, fixing fence or clearing land then everyone ate their sack lunches together. As a child, these special eating arrangements seemed kind of like a picnic to me. My lunch usually consisted of two sandwiches, a 5-cent package of Potato Chips, maybe an apple or banana, and, if lucky, a homemade fried apple or peach pie.

Looking back I have come to appreciate the uniqueness of the Hot Link Joint. At the time, those of us eating together were unaware we were participating in a radical social experiment on the cutting edge of change.

A Hot Link Joint Today

The Hot Link Joint has evolved over the decades so that today it resembles an ordinary restaurant with a more modern atmosphere. Air conditioning has replaced the ceiling fans. You still see the benches and counter but they are now more a token of the past because modern booths are also provided. Nothing remains inside the square counter area so customers now sit on both sides when the place is crowded. The hot links, drinks, butcher paper, crackers, hot sauce, cash register, waitresses and now deserts and some new dishes such as chili are located in a controlled serving line in the back of the establishment.

Special dishes such as hamburgers, french-fries, and breakfast are prepared in a separate kitchen. Now you can even buy a healthy green salad. But the biggest difference is that people now sit wherever they like.

The lowly Hot Link Joint was the place of a social experiment even though we didn't know it. The Hot Link Joint somehow escaped classification as a real restaurant and consequently was exempted from the rigid restaurant rules. For whatever reason, social or economic, Hot Link Joints didn't post signs "For Whites Only." Whites and blacks ate in the same restaurant, in the same room, and around one counter.

Today, all public places in my hometown are equally open to whites and blacks and few remember how it was. Therefore, I have declared victory for my hometown in the front-street and back-street social war about race. However, prejudice can still draw invisible lines. Invisible lines still run through the hearts of men in old and new forms.

WHY DO SOME ACT AND OTHERS REMAIN SILENT?

STORY 17

Special Friends

*Being a Negro in America means trying to smile
when you want to cry. It means trying to hold on to
physical life amid psychological death. It means
the pain of watching your children grow up with
clouds of inferiority in their mental skies.*
Martin Luther King Jr.
Where Do We Go from Here: Chaos or Community? 1967.

Some of my warmest and most cherished memories are associated with a special group of Black friends. I still feel a deep emotional attachment to Lou Vella Stanberry, Hooks Lawton, and S. White. I also think often about Booker T. Bell, one of these friends nearer my age.

These cherished relationships with the Black friends and mentors in my life seem to be warmer and etched more deeply into my heart than others. They were special and close to me, yet we were separated from large portions of each other's worlds. I have searched to understand what was so special about these relationships. Why are they embedded so deeply into my good memories? Why have these memories survived for decades while others have faded?

My relationship to these friends had a special childlike quality on both sides. I now realize they could relate to me as a White child in ways they could never relate in the White adult world. As a child, I could relate to them in a way forbidden to an adult. They showed affection and kindness to me as we operated in a social order that demanded they treat me, a child, with a type of adult respect. They touched me deep down in my purest and simplest emotions, but there was a point beyond which we could not go because of the rules of society.

In spite of, or maybe because of their circumstances, they possessed dignity and warmth that has remained with me for more than seven decades. Looking back I am amazed at the absence of bitterness. Of course, I know they felt pain from the indignities, but they seemed to live beyond bitterness. These dear friends lived out the philosophy of Dr. King before he was even born. "I have decided to stick with love. Hate is too great a burden to bear."

Jesus taught the same: "Love your enemies, do good to those who hate you, bless those who curse you, pray for those who mistreat you." My dear Black friends lived out that verse every day.

Lou Vella

Lou Vella Stanberry is one of my best childhood memories. She became our full-time housekeeper and cook (our maid) because my mother continued to teach 1st Grade after my father returned from WWII.

Lou Vella was a wonderful cook and I can still taste her hot water corn bread, chicken fried steak and gravy, peach cobbler and Eagle Brand Lemon Ice Box pie. To make her even more special to me, she almost always took my side in disputes with my older brother. I was sure Lou Vella loved me just like I was one of her own children. I don't know that for sure but I surely felt that way. She was a second mother to me.

My parents always treated Lou Vella with personal respect and dignity. However, she went home to her little house in "Happy Hollow," attended her own church, operated on the back street of business, was restricted to low paying jobs, and sent her children to separate schools. She was part of our family and yet not part of our society. Only on special occasions, such as weddings and funerals, was she allowed to enter our social and religious world.

Lou Vella sat with our family in our church at the funeral of my preacher grandfather in 1954 and shared our grief at the death of my older brother in November of 1955. She was only marginally part of our political world and could vote between the white candidates that were chosen to run for offices by white Democrats.

Our religious worlds operated in different parts of town as well. She was a wonderful Christian and loved to attend St. Beulah C.M.E (Colored Methodist Episcopal) Church. I was part of the First Baptist Church where one of my great-great-grandfathers had served as pastor from 1870 to 1874.

Riding in the Back Seat

In her own way, Lou Vella was part of the civil rights movement sweeping across the South. She attended various kinds of civil rights meetings in our town that in my Mother's thinking, "stirred her up." Rosa Parks, the 42-year old seamstress who refused to give her seat on a bus to a White man, inspired Lou Vella. Rosa Parks' arrest and fine sparked the 381-day Montgomery Bus Boycott when most of the Black community walked rather than rode the public buses. The economic boycott eventually forced the bus companies to open its seating and to hire Black bus drivers. This event catapulted the young pastor of Dexter Avenue Baptist Church, Martin Luther King, Jr., into national prominence.

In fact, Lou Vella reminds me of Rosa Parks. Both were small women with quiet determination and both were dedicated members of the African Methodist Episcopal Church. The closest Lou Vella ever came to protest with me was one Saturday afternoon when I was home from college. She always rode up in the front seat with me whenever I drove her home after work. However, this Saturday afternoon, she refused to ride in the front seat and made a point of getting into the back seat.

She had been doing this for several weeks with my Mother as a protest because employers did not give Social Security benefits to their maids. Of course my parents helped Lou financially beyond her salary when she had special needs or emergencies. My mother always gave Lou a birthday and Christmas gift along with a Christmas bonus. I know Lou Vella appreciated their generosity. However, Lou Vella wanted her rights as a citizen and not just gifts that came from the generosity of someone. Riding in the back seat of the car was her way of making her views known to "Miss Julia." It was a Rosa Parks protest in reverse. Lou's back-seat-treatment of us was to let us know she was experiencing back-seat-things from our world. It was not so much about money as about rights, dignity and fairness. Eventually she received her Social Security benefits. My mother kept giving the presents and bonus as well.

Lou Vella never resigned herself to the caste system in which society had placed her. She may not have been empowered by the culture but she was empowered by a dignity that came directly from her relationship with God. Dr. King shares the story of a seventy-two-year-old woman in Montgomery, Alabama "who rose up with a sense of dignity and with her people decided not to ride segregated buses, and who responded with ungrammatical profundity to one who inquired about her weariness: 'My feets is tired, but my soul is at rest.'"

This was the spirit of Lou Vella Stanberry.

WHY DO SOME ACT AND OTHERS REMAIN SILENT?

STORY 18

Friends: Lightning & S. White

*The arc of the moral universe is long,
but it bends toward justice.*
Theodore Parker
Often quoted by Martin Luther King, Jr.

We called Hooks Lawton, Lightning. He was tagged with this reverse nickname because his 6-foot 2-inch slender frame and natural athletic grace gave him the appearance of always moving slowly. In his community, his name was associated with his lightning quick fastball. Lightning worked for my Father for fifteen years as the "mud man" or "mortar man." The "mud man" made the mortar for the bricklayers in our Briggs & Stratton cement mixer and was a very important person on the job. If the mortar was not mixed properly with just the right portions of Trinity mix (one 70-pound sack), masonry river sand (16 to 18 full shovels), and water (2 full buckets) then the bricklayer's work was affected. This was no easy task when sometimes as many as five to ten bricklayers were on the job laying 800-1000 brick per person per day. My dad's business would shut down without Lightning.

During World War I, Lightning pitched for one of the Army Service Baseball Teams. Most of the outstanding baseball players were drafted during World War I and so the Service Teams were probably better than the professional teams left playing in the United States. Therefore, the fact that he could pitch at that level confirms he had talent at the professional level.

He and all the other Black workers loved the Los Angeles Dodgers because Jackie Robinson was the first Black star to play in the Majors in the modern era, and he played for the Dodgers. I was a Micky Mantle, Yogi Berra and Whitey Ford Yankees fan. During the 1953 World Series between the Dodgers and Yankees, Lightning commented: "I was born too early. If I had been born later, I would have pitched in the Major Leagues." Many in the Black community who had seen him pitch in his prime agreed. However, Lightning was working for my father as our "mud man" for a little above minimum wage.

S. White

S. White's mother gave him the name "S". That is the only name he had, and that is the name we wrote on his check. When he reported for World War I the soldier in charge asked him his name. He replied: "S White." The soldier barked: "What does the "S" stand for?" He replied: "That's all of my name and it doesn't stand for anything else." The soldier exploded and said, "In this man's army you must have a name! Your name will be Samuel White." So, all through the Great War "S" was "Samuel." After his discharge, he went back to just plain "S".

Each summer I spent eight hours a day and five days a week working with S White. Because manpower rather than machine power was used for as many construction jobs as possible, S and I dug ditches for foundations, prepared floors to pour concrete slabs, carried brick, shoveled mortar and did all other kinds of necessary jobs.

S was born sometime near the turn of the century and so was already a middle-aged man at that time. However, he could work me to death even when I was in shape to play football.

If we started at opposite ends of a ditch I would go just as fast as I could fighting to use the pick and shovel, trying to beat him past the middle. I would look up to see how he was doing. He would be methodically using the pick and shovel, never missing a beat and never making a wasted motion. It was always embarrassing because I could never outwork S.

He was a distinguished gentleman with beautiful silver hair. I remember how neat S was with his personal appearance, his little rent house, and the sack lunch he brought to eat at noon.

Indignities

From time to time my father's work crew ate at a café rather than bringing sack lunches. That is when I became aware of the indignity our Black workers endured. Lightning and S., along with the other Black workers, weren't allowed to eat with us. They could try to find a Black café in the area but often there was none within walking distance and we didn't have time to drive to two places. Therefore, my father ordered a meal at the white restaurant and took their plates of food out to them, or sometimes they could eat "in the back in the kitchen." It never made sense to me as a boy that we ate sack lunches together and didn't eat together in restaurants.

Another incident helped me realize our Black workers not only faced indignity but also danger. One summer my father was building a basketball gymnasium in a small community far back in the bottoms about 20 miles north of my hometown. One narrow road with the longest wooden bridge I ever saw connected Sugar Hill to the outside world. When cars approached from opposite directions, one car had to wait until the other crossed. If two cars met on the bridge, one had to back out. I was always relieved when our red Chevrolet pickup got to the end of that groaning and swaying bridge.

This small community was shut off from the outside world. Its customs and values were frozen in the past. There were no fences and all the livestock ran wild. The cattle were branded and ear notches identified the hogs. Horses were still a primary means of transportation and were tied to hitching posts throughout the one-general-store town. A Ku Klux Klan mentality remained. No Blacks lived in Sugar Hill and the town had the reputation of carefully monitoring a Black who crossed the bridge and of taking action if he lingered.

My father thought it best not to take his Black workers on this job. He had my brother and me to help as laborers and he hired enough local workers to take care of the eight or nine bricklayers necessary to lay the four twelve-inch thick brick walls that were long enough, wide enough, and high enough for a basketball court and bleachers. We needed Lightning because he was the "mud man." Therefore, my father assured him that he would be safe with us in Sugar Hill. However, I can still see the concern in his eyes all the time we were there. Lightning always seemed to breathe a sigh of relief when we crossed back to the other side of that wooden bridge.

WHY DO SOME ACT AND OTHERS REMAIN SILENT?

STORY 19

Friends: Booker T. Bell & Juneteenth

*Discrimination is a hellhound that gnaws at
Negroes in every waking moment of their lives to
remind them that the lie of their inferiority is
accepted as truth in the society dominating them.*
Martin Luther King Jr.
Atlanta, August 16, 1967

Booker T. Bell, one of my Father's construction workers, was short, stout and strong as an ox with an infectious smile and a fun-loving spirit. I was about ten years younger than Booker T. and had worked along-side of him for several years. Booker T. was married and had children. I was unmarried and had just graduated from college. Despite the difference in our ages and circumstances, I considered Booker T. to be a friend and this caused me to be even more surprised by our work conflict on Juneteenth 1960.

Juneteenth is a combination of the date, "June" and "nineteenth." Growing up I didn't celebrate this holiday and didn't think much about it. I knew this day was special to the black community in my hometown. On this day, everyone in "colored town" dressed up in their Sunday best, cooked special dishes and celebrated, or they celebrated as soon as they got off from work. They treated the day like the Fourth of July, and I wasn't sure why anyone needed another Fourth of July.

When Juneteenth fell on Saturday or Sunday everyone was happy. However, there was tension when Juneteenth fell on a weekday because Juneteenth was not an official holiday. Since the work force was mostly Black, tension always built up as we approached the date for the celebration of Juneteenth. The work force wanted the day off, but the bosses, like my Dad with his construction business, only shut down for official holidays such as Thanksgiving, Christmas, Easter, and July 4th.

The Origins of Juneteenth

President Lincoln freed almost 4 million slaves when he signed The Emancipation Proclamation on January 1, 1863. However, the Proclamation had little immediate effect on the day-to-day lives of slaves, particularly in Texas where the Confederates were almost entirely in control. Emancipation only became a reality after the war ended.

On June 19, 1865 the Union General, Gordon Granger, and 2,000 federal troops arrived on Galveston Island to take possession of the state, to enforce the slaves' new freedoms, and to begin reconstructing the economic, political and social structures of the South.

Slaves in Galveston rejoiced in the streets with jubilant celebrations and Juneteenth was born. Over the next several years, the freed slaves in Texas celebrated this day and purchased land so they would have places to accommodate the increasingly large Juneteenth gatherings. These celebrations spread to other states and became an unofficial holiday tradition.

In 1980, Juneteenth became an official state holiday in Texas. Thirteen other states now list it as an official holiday, including New York, New Jersey, Connecticut, Alaska, and California. However, one hundred years after the Emancipation Proclamation, Juneteenth in Texas in 1960, in my hometown and on my Dad's construction job was still unofficial.

A Juneteenth Conflict

We were building an office for Arkla Gas Company in my hometown. It was Texas hot with no shade and Juneteenth fell on Friday that year. My Dad had a large crew of bricklayers and laborers hard at work and left me in charge of the crew of laborers because he had to be away during the day for a meeting.

After my Dad left, I noticed Booker T. and one of the temporary workers, who was a tall former basketball player, were dissatisfied, sullen and doing as little work as possible. The word around the job was that they were upset because they had to work on Juneteenth.

When we broke for lunch, short and stout Booker T. and the tall basketball player walked the short distance into town and returned thirty or forty minutes late. I could tell they had probably had a drink or two on the way and I confronted them about being late. They quit on the spot. I can still see them walking together back toward town and the Juneteenth celebration.

At the time, I found it difficult to understand why Booker T. reacted the way he did. I felt he took advantage of me when I was in charge of the crew. I didn't have a clue about the deeper meaning of the tension about Juneteenth.

I was a prime example of blissful ignorance that can unconsciously perpetuate social injustice. I grew up with these men but did not comprehend the social dynamics that made Juneteenth so important to them.

I now understand that the issue was more than just having a day off. However, in 1960, I was ignorant of its importance to Booker T., and probably to the other laborers who kept working in silent resignation.

The Spirit of Juneteenth

Maybe part of Booker T.'s motive was to just get a day off and to have a holiday. Booker T. did like to have a good time. However, I now believe other forces were working deep down within him of which I was ignorant. For Booker T., Juneteenth was a reminder that the promise of the Emancipation Proclamation still remained unfulfilled after 100 years.

In the words of Martin Luther King: "the hellhound of discrimination was gnawing" at the guts of Booker T. and I was clueless to the social forces, resentments, and indignities at work deep within him. Incredible changes that neither Booker T. nor I could imagine, were already in progress when the Juneteenth standoff took place. However, the social ignorance of people like me had to be exposed and changed before the original intent of Lincoln's Emancipation Proclamation could become reality one hundred years later.

Booker T. was wrong in the specific issue (being late for work, drinking while working, and poor work) but he was right in the broader issue of injustice, unfairness and prejudice. I may have been right in the specific issue but I was wrong in the most important factors of fairness, justice and empathy.

I was an excellent example of the warning of Dr. King: "Nothing in all the world is more dangerous than sincere ignorance and conscientious stupidity."

WHY DO SOME ACT AND OTHERS REMAIN SILENT?

STORY 20

Code of Courtesy

The Negro's great stumbling block in the drive
toward freedom is . . . the white moderate who
is more devoted to order than to justice.
Martin Luther King Jr.
April 16, 1963, Letter from a Birmingham Jail.

I was surprised to overhear a cantankerous old bricklayer complaining to my Father. "Jimmie, James Spence and Bill are saying 'Yes Sir' and 'No Sir' to Lightning and S. You need to tell them to stop!"

My father responded forcefully to this man he had known for decades. "Bittie! Leave James Spence and Bill alone. They are doing exactly what they have been taught." "They have been taught to say 'Yes Sir' and 'No Sir' to all adults and that includes Lightning and S."

He shared this conversation with my mother that night when he thought my brother and I weren't listening. From their reaction to this incident, I learned that my parents believed every person had God-given dignity that required respect, courtesy, and politeness.

"Good" people in the south applied an unwritten code of courtesy even to relationships between the races. The code of courtesy had been maintained during slavery and was continued during segregation. For adults, the code of courtesy was an outward veneer of politeness that was intended to cover up ugly prejudice. However, as a child, the code of courtesy worked in my life in an entirely different way. It was a seed of fairness planted in my heart. It became a lens through which I began to see my world.

Separate but Equal

My father was hired in 1949 to brick veneer most of the wooden buildings on the Douglass School campus, the segregated Black school. The project included the administration offices, several classroom buildings, and the construction of a new gymnasium. The Pittsburg Gazette reported that the cost was an estimated $10,000.

This was done to satisfy the "separate but equal" clause in the Supreme Court's ruling about education that had been handed down in Plessy v. Ferguson in 1896. The doctrine would be overturned in 1954 in Brown v. Board of Education. However, in 1949, society was still trying to maintain the façade of "separate but equal."

The summer of 1949 I was ten and my older brother and I began helping our father on his construction jobs that summer because our mother began her Master's study in Elementary Education.

We took water to the bricklayers, carried a few bricks, and fetched tools. That first summer we could lie down under a shade tree if we got tired. However, by the next summer we were expected to keep busy all day long.

While working on the Black campus that first summer, I joined in a pickup baseball game with a group of the neighborhood kids in a vacant lot next to the school. I was impressed with their speed, agility, and passion for the game.

I remembered this a few years later when I was a senior in High School and part of the track team. During one of our practices,

Coach Clark told us that a ninth grader at Douglass High, the Black school, was timed in less than 10 seconds flat in the one-hundred-yard dash. We had one of the top sprinters in Texas and he wasn't running that fast. We laughed that their stopwatch was broken.

Later we found out the ninth-grade boy was Homer Jones who eventually ran on the all Black Texas Southern University track team that set national and world records. He also was an All Pro end with the New York Giants football team.

Professor Hartsell Lampkin was Supervising Principal, really the Superintendent of Douglass School. Mr. Fred Colvin was the white superintendent of all of the Pittsburg School District that included Douglass. Professor D. M. Smith was the Principle of Douglass High School.

We observed the code of courtesy with Mr. Lampkin and Professor Smith. My Father respectfully called them "Mister" or "Professor" and, of course, I always said "Yes Sir" and "No Sir" to them. To me they were impressive African American authority figures.

However, even at the age of ten I was shocked by the condition of the Black school facilities. The new red brick on the outside could not blot out what I saw on the inside. Looking through the windows I saw desks, chalk boards and books that I knew were hand me downs from the white school.

This experience was the first crack in seeing through the code of courtesy for me. When I said "Yes Sir" and "No Sir" to Mr. Lampkin and Professor Smith, and other Blacks, I was giving equal respect. However, what I saw inside the buildings didn't match up to the outside respect,

That summer of my life I began to wonder, "Why do we then treated them as second class? Why must these kids attend a school that receive less than our school?"

Federal Troops and the Opening of School

In the fall of 1957, the Federal Courts ordered the integration of Central High School in Little Rock, Arkansas and the local authorities defied the court order. President Eisenhower federalized the Arkansas National Guard and sent 1000 U.S. Army paratroopers of the 101st Airborne to enforce the integration of the school.

In a visit home during my second year of college, I watched the historic scene unfold on our black and white television set during the noon news. In the newsreel, Black students walked through a howling white mob with the Federal troops in full battle gear restraining the hate with their presence and their guns. One woman still sticks out in my mind because her face was filled with ugly hate and anger as she taunted the Black students.

Gov. Faubus of Arkansas stood in defiance on the high steps of the largest high school in the state. This inspired Gov. Barnett of Mississippi to do the same thing at the University of Mississippi. Gov. George Wallace of Alabama then followed with his declaration at the University of Alabama: "Segregation now, segregation tomorrow, and segregation forever."

A code of courtesy had given an appearance of decorum in the South while maintaining a segregated system. However, television exposed the hypocrisy of the code of courtesy during the Civil Rights Movement and the integration of the public schools. The mob scenes on TV that day and the response of these governors destroyed that perception forever.

As we watched the ugly events at Little Rock, I strongly disagreed with my Father about an important issue for the first time. I told him that the school situation between the whites and blacks "was not fair" and that the doctrine of "separate but equal" was a joke. I brought up the situation we had seen with our own eyes when we had worked on the Black campus seven or eight years earlier. I reminded him of the inferiority of the buildings and how the desks and books were "hand me downs" from our school. My parting statement was: "If I were Black, I would be marching and protesting also."

My father did not get angry with me. I believe he knew the unfairness of the political and social systems in our world. However, he had a hard time balancing order and justice. In his mind, you should respect a person as a person but must also respect the law as the law. In his thinking, disorder was disrespect for the law, even when the law was not yet fair and equal.

Dr. King understood the tension between order and justice. "I have almost reached the regrettable conclusion that the Negro's great stumbling block in his stride toward freedom is not the White Citizen's Councilor or the Ku Klux Klanner, but the white moderate, who is more devoted to 'order' than to justice . . ." He concluded: "Shallow understanding from people of good will is more frustrating than absolute misunderstanding from people of ill will. Lukewarm acceptance is much more bewildering than outright rejection."

WHY DO SOME ACT AND OTHERS REMAIN SILENT?

STORY 21

WHAT IF . . .?

Our lives begin to end the day we
become silent about things that matter.
Martin Luther King Jr.
March 8, 1965, Paraphrase from a speech after *Bloody Sunday*.

I chose the topic of "segregation and integration" for my first college research paper. It was the spring of 1957, and I was in Mrs. Huggins English 101 class. During my research, I discovered disturbing articles in *Time Magazine* and the *Dallas Morning News* about Dr. W. A. Criswell, pastor of the First Baptist Church of Dallas, the largest church in Texas at that time. Criswell was a well-known preacher in the United States, and a leader among Southern Baptists.

On February 21, 1956, Dr. Criswell preached at the South Carolina Baptist Evangelism Conference. He began with a challenging message about evangelism, a subject dear to the heart of Baptists. However, he soon began a heated attack on the forces of desegregation. Some of his language was crude and demeaning to the black community.

Governor Timmerman of South Carolina, a member of a Baptist Church, invited Criswell to address the State Legislature the next day. United States Senator Strom Thurman, who had run for the Presidency in 1948 as the segregationist Dixiecrat candidate, introduced him.

The next year, Senator Thurman conducted the longest filibuster in the history of the United States Senate. He spoke for more than 24 hours non-stop in opposition to the Civil Rights Act of 1957. In this politically charged atmosphere, Dr. Criswell repeated, before the South Carolina legislature, the harsh message of the previous day.

De Facto Segregation

For much of the national news media, Dr. Criswell's rhetoric established Southern Baptists as the *de facto* segregated church of the South. After all, he was pastor of the largest Southern Baptist Church in the country, was speaking in South Carolina, the "cradle of the Confederacy," and was introduced by the best-known segregationist politician in the government.

In addition, Dr. Criswell denounced as "foolishness" and "idiocy" the recent ruling of the Supreme Court that was meant to "ram integration down the collective throat of the South." He was talking about the 1954 Supreme Court decision of Brown v. Board of Education. Some Baptist leaders sought to repair the damage to the reputation of the denomination. *Time Magazine* quoted one leader who declared: "Criswell is not the pope of Southern Baptists."

I was deeply embarrassed by his position and in the paper took a strong position for integrating our public schools and churches. Mrs. Huggins critiqued my paper in her office in the beautiful Armstrong Browning Building at Baylor University. "Your paper is very good, but too short." "You have a strong writing style." She also added a word of encouragement. "You obviously feel strongly about this issue. Continue to live out your convictions."

Twelve years later, after the major battles about the race issue had been fought and when he was a candidate for President of the Southern Baptist Convention, Dr. Criswell wept as he apologized publicly on several occasions for his past attitude about African Americans.

Fearing public exposure and humiliation, the water fountains and rest rooms in the Texas Baptist headquarters in Dallas were finally quietly desegregated. During this time, other denominational leaders also began to apologize for their silence.

What Kind of People Worship Here?

During one of his stays in jail, Dr. King reflected on the church in the South and the Civil Rights Movement. In a letter to eight white pastors, he discussed the White churches, Christians, and Christian leaders. He acknowledged the glory and power of the church in the South.

> *I have traveled the length and breadth of Alabama, Mississippi and all the other southern states. On sweltering summer days and crisp autumn mornings I have looked at the South's beautiful churches with their lofty spires pointing heavenward. I have beheld the impressive outlines of her massive religious education buildings.*

However, in the letter, Dr. King asked some disturbing questions about the church in the South.

> *What kind of people worships here? Who is their God? Where were their voices when the lips of Governor Barnett dripped with words of interposition and nullification? Where were they when Governor Wallace gave a clarion call for defiance and hatred? Where were their voices of support when bruised and weary Negro men and women decided to rise from the dark dungeons of complacency to the bright hills of creative protest?*

What if . . .?

As a child of the South, I am haunted by the historical possibility of "what might have been." What if the church had lived out God's command to love and care for the poor, weak and helpless during the early history of the United States, during the time before the Civil War, and during the one hundred years that followed?

Consider the first one hundred years of the United States. The Church moved west with the expansion of the country. Churches of all kinds, but especially Baptist and Methodist, were soon present in almost every village, town, and city in the South from Virginia to Texas. What if just the Baptist and Methodist churches had lived out the teachings of Jesus about love instead of mirroring the social, political and economic slave culture of the day?

I believe these churches could have changed history. Millions of Black men, women and children could have enjoyed freedom. 640,000 men would not have died in the War Between the States. The United States would have escaped the tragedy of debasing the dream of living out the truth that "all men are created equal." If the Church had been willing to pay the price of living out Biblical ethics, the terrible cost in human lives and dignity would have been avoided.

Even if the church had failed to pay the price during the first one hundred years (1760-1860), there was the choice during the next one hundred years (1865-1965). In the years that followed the Civil War, what if these same churches had repented, reconciled and spoken out against segregation that continued as a form of social, political and economic intolerance? What if these churches had denounced hate organizations such as the Ku Klux Klan?

Through the church, I believe the freedom bought by blood during the Revolutionary War, decreed by law in the Constitution, and fought for during the Civil War could have been a reality for the one hundred years after the Civil War.

The quote by Edger Allen Poe expresses the tragedy of the church concerning slavery and segregation. "The saddest word of tongue or pen are truly these . . . . .It might have been.'"

Why Do Some Act and Others Remain Silent?

STORY 22

Three Pastors: Methodist, Catholic & Baptist

*We will have to repent in this generation
not merely for the vitriolic words and
action of the bad people but for the
appalling silence of the good people.*
Martin Luther King
April 16, 1963, Letter from Birmingham Jail

Mark Lewis was pastor of the First Methodist Church, Father Ed Haggerty was the Catholic priest, and I was pastor of the First Baptist Church. God placed us together in a small East Texas town that was forced to integrate the public-school system and to come to grips with 100 years of systemic segregation. Father Haggerty was already serving in the community when I arrived and Mark Lewis followed me by a year.

I came to admire and appreciate these two pastors as we sought to deal with the ethical dilemma that had been passed down through history to this particular time and place. We knew God expected us to do what we could to help change the status quo of a hundred years of segregation that followed a hundred years of slavery.

Ministerial Alliance

For the first time, the local Ministerial Alliance began meeting monthly with all the pastors in the county, including the Black pastors. Reverend Pinky Beckham was one of the pastors of one of the Black churches. When he prayed in the pastor's group in his pictorial language, he took all of us up to heaven and brought heaven down to us. Because we shared the same last name, we joked about being relatives.

The uncomfortable truth is that we may have had a "family" name connection. Sadly, several of my ancestors owned slaves and fought in the Civil War. I have a copy of the Last Will & Testament of one of my great-grandfathers that is dated January 1, 1865. In the document, he freed his slaves and made provision for them.

I am struck by one personal comment my great-grandfather included in his Will. "I never broke up any of the families or sold them separately." My great-grandfather evidently wanted to believe in levels of guilt and wrong, and I would like to believe that for him as well. I would like to think this Will is a testament to his ethical conversion about the evil institution of slavery. Unfortunately, I cannot fairly evaluate his actions because he wrote this Will just five months before the Civil War ended in 1865. He made this decision to free his slaves only after a terrible war that cost more than 600,000 lives and destroyed the political and economic culture of the thirteen Southern States of America that supported his right to be a slave owner. Therefore, as it is with all of us, only God can judge levels of culpability.

The irony of fighting civil rights battles with a Black pastor with the same surname of Beckham did not escape me. It reminded me that I was still living in a segregated town with segregated churches because many of my ancestors fought to maintain a segregated society.

Parades and Politics

Our simple decision to integrate the Ministerial Alliance led to several other actions and reactions. Each year during the first week in May, the town had a Pilgrimage. Tourists came from all over Texas to see the antebellum homes and buildings and to participate in special activities that celebrated the past history of the town as a steamboat center that shipped cotton and other goods from Texas to New Orleans.

The celebration was kicked off with a parade that was traditionally led by the local pastors. The first year Mark Lewis, Ed Haggerty and I were together as pastors in the town, we walked at the front of the parade with the Black pastors. As far as I know, no one said anything negative to any of us about inviting the Black pastors to be part of the parade. However, the remaining three years I was in the town, the pastors were never invited to march at the head of the parade again.

As tensions began to grow, we convinced the County Judge, Sheriff, School Superintendent and other county officials to meet monthly with us and the leaders of the Black community in an effort to promote dialogue and diffuse tension. The county officials were willing to do this because it benefited them politically in the midst of what could escalate into major conflict. Also, these elected officials and their families were members of the Methodist, Catholic and Baptist churches where Mark Lewis, Ed Haggerty and I served as pastors.

Public Forum

The summer before the local public-school system was integrated in the fall, the Ministerial Alliance sponsored a Forum for parents to discuss the approaching public school integration. The well-attended meeting took place in our new community center that had been built "across the tracks" with a government grant in one of the poorer sections of town. I moderated the meeting from a table that was positioned exactly in the center aisle that divided the two sections. The white parents sat on my right and the Black parents on my left. Father Haggerty sat beside me as moral support.

After an opening prayer, we established the ground rules for the meeting: recognition from the moderator was required before speaking, civil courtesy would be maintained, no personal attacks and only one person speaking at a time. The wife of the County Attorney stood up and began to speak angrily and emotionally about her fear that the quality of education would suffer and that the lack of discipline in the schools would create an unsafe environment. I saw on her face the same angry and ugly expression that I had seen fifteen years before. It was the face of the jeering woman in the crowd that blocked the way of the Black students integrating Central High School in Little Rock, Arkansas in 1957.

From that point, it looked like the meeting was going to deteriorate into ugly accusations and insinuations. I recognized a stately Black father of about 40 years of age. He stood up on the left side of the aisle and calmly shared his heart. "I want my children to learn and to behave and I will see that they respect teachers and other students." His wisdom and humility changed the discussion at that point from a fight over the institution of segregation, to something personal. The conversation was now between parents about their passion for education and their children.

That year the integration of the public-school system took place with much tension and difficulty but without bloodshed or too many embarrassing incidents. Our twin sons, Joey and Jimmy, were part of the first integrated class in the history of the school and Mary, my wife, taught Special Education for a year during that time.

Looking back I know God worked in a special way in that specific town, during a difficult period of history, through a

Methodist pastor, a Catholic priest and a Baptist preacher. However, these memories are also painful. Painful because the memories remind me just how deeply racism was ingrained in the systems and hearts of people in towns and cities all across our land.

STORY 23

PHONE CALLS & HANDSHAKES

If physical death is the price that I must pay to free my white brothers and sisters from a permanent death of the spirit, then nothing can be more redemptive.
Martin Luther King
June 5, 1964, After hearing of threats to his life.

One Saturday morning during the height of racial tension, I sat at my desk completing the preparation of two sermons for Sunday. The phone rang and a voice spoke to me in an exaggerated "Southern black" dialect. "Pastor, I hears that Mt. Zion Baptist Church needs a pastor. I think you needs to become their pastor." I tried to recognize the voice of the older white man with the fake "Black" accent. Mt. Zion was a Black Church. I replied, "I would be glad to pastor that church if God wants me to, and if the members will have me." "Who is this?" Silence! Then I heard the click as the phone went dead.

That "click" represents the silent intimidation used to maintain segregation and that made Sunday morning at 11:00 the most segregated meeting in the United States. The unwritten rule of survival for most pastors in the South was: "Don't preach about race from the pulpit."

The Parable of the Good Samaritan

During the period of time of the phone call, I was preaching a Sunday morning sermon series on the Parables of Jesus. As the time approached to preach on the Parable of the Good Samaritan, I was faced with a choice. I could preach about

Jesus' beautiful lesson of helping people in need and stop there, or I could apply Jesus' other truth about prejudice. The Jews had a deep prejudice toward the Samaritans and considered them to be an inferior race.

This was a favorite parable among Black preachers such as Dr. King. Everyone shared a popular sermon outline. "The first question which the priest and the Levite asked was: 'If I stop to help this man, what will happen to *me*?' But the Good Samaritan reversed the question: 'If I do not stop to help this man, what will happen to *him*?'"

Jesus' parable forced me to ask myself "how can I ignore the spiritual truth of prejudice in the Parable of the Good Samaritan in light of the social and political situation of the church and community?" I eventually prepared a message that addressed both the truth about helping those in physical need and loving those in need of equal respect. I used a familiar outline to explain the attitudes of three of the characters in the story. The Robbers (Takers): "What is yours is mine I will take it." The Priest and the Levite (Keepers): "What is mine is mine I will keep it." The Samaritan (Givers): "What is mine (aid or respect) is yours I will share it."

I still remember the dynamics surrounding that sermon. I went through agony in preparing the words I would speak about prejudice. I wanted to speak the truth, but I wanted to speak the truth in love. That was not easy because I was filled with a certain amount of righteous anger about things like ugly phone calls and hate letters. I knew my anger could lead me to speak the right message with the wrong spirit. I desperately needed humility because I was condemning the lifestyle of an entire community along with the culture of my birth.

I remember my concern was not only about what discrimination by Whites was doing to Black Americans. I also voiced my concern about what discrimination had done and was doing to my soul and the soul of my church members and our society. This sermon was about us, about our attitude toward others and about our position before God. Martin Luther King saw this danger for the soul of the white man. "The Negro needs the white man to free him from his fears. The white man needs the Negro to free him from his guilt."

The consequences of my actions also weighed heavily upon me. The deacons in this Baptist Church could recommend that the congregation fire me. I was preparing myself for the humiliation of being asked to leave. I wondered: "What other Baptist church will want to hire a trouble-making preacher?" I felt alone, fearful and vulnerable as I stood before my church members that Sunday morning. It was not fear necessarily about physical harm as much as fear of rejection.

The sermon created the reaction that I feared. No one walked out but I could see anger on the face of some and disappointment on the face of others. They were upset because I was preaching one more time about the taboo subject of race. I was thankful for a few friendly faces who I knew supported what I was saying.

Handshakes

I felt an oppressive tension as the choir sang the benediction. Feeling like a condemned man, I walked to the entrance of the church for the traditional greetings, handshakes, and perfunctory "Preacher I enjoyed the sermon." However, nothing was perfunctory about this day. Some of the people made their displeasure known by refusing to shake my hand. Others shook my hand without enthusiasm or comment. Some kept far enough away from the line that they were able to slip past without even making eye contact. A few escaped out the back door. Those who slept through the sermon didn't know what happened until they got to their car.

Fortunately, in some way, seeds of change were planted. I can still see Bennie coming out the door that Sunday morning and offering his hand with a wide grin. He was a big, good-natured, and pre-maturely white-haired man who operated several lumber trucks that transported logs to sawmills. Bennie used many black laborers in his work and got just as dirty as his crew, but he was a very sharp dresser on Sunday. He was a good boss, but operated with the old system of relationships. I knew his handshake and grin was not an endorsement of my views or a conversion about the wrongs of racial prejudice. It just meant he would indulge my sermon, but it wouldn't change him. At least he was grinning. Several years later God did transform Bennie's life. Later in life he would share his moving testimony, specifically about how God had dramatically changed his attitudes about black people.

I was not surprised when George gave me a sincere handshake of approval and support. He was a six-foot four-inch Louisiana born Cajun who weighed about 280 pounds when on a rigid diet. He was an ex-Marine who had carried his prejudice with him for years in and out of the service. We became fishing buddies during a time God was changing his life. I knew God's work in him was deep and genuine because it removed his prejudice.

Sometime after my Good Samaritan sermon, George walked upon a big commotion in the center of downtown. A large car with two older Black couples was trying to parallel park. A young white woman in a pickup truck was behind the car angrily honking her horn and yelling out the window. The people in the car were yelling back at the woman in the truck that they were trying to parallel park. Neither would yield and a crowd was gathering.

George walked up to the car, bent down, and looked in the front passenger window. The face of this huge white man startled the occupants of the car. With a smile on his face George spoke: "Won't it be wonderful when we get to heaven and don't have to put up with this mess?" After the shock wore off, they all broke into wide grins and shouted, "Hallelujah!" "Amen!" Then they drove off laughing.

Knowing that my stand about race might eventually affect the attitudes of people like Bennie and George would have made the experience a little less painful and stressful.

Although it was painfully slow, change in the right direction was happening in the hearts and lives of some.

WHY DO SOME ACT AND OTHERS REMAIN SILENT?

STORY 24

UGLY WORDS IN A DEACONS MEETING

*A good many observers have remarked that if
equality could come at once the Negro would
not be ready for it. I submit that the white
American is even more unprepared.*
Martin Luther King Jr., 1963

A short time after my Good Samaritan sermon, the church was considering the purchase of an adjacent piece of property that would give additional parking. The price was good and the church was growing, so the purchase made good strategic and business sense. A committee, chaired by one of our young and progressive deacons, had studied the pros and cons of purchasing the property.

The chairman of the committee was giving the final committee report at our regular monthly Deacons Meeting. I knew the recommendation would be to purchase the property and this usually meant the deacons and the church would adopt the proposal.

We met in the special room where the deacons had considered the business of the church for years. I sat on the right side of the speaker in the front row next to the outside wall. About 20 deacons sat behind me in four or five rows of chairs.

The chairman of the committee was making the case that using the two-story building on the property for a Youth Center was one of the advantages of the deal.

Muttering

During the report, I heard some under-the-breath muttering that was intentionally loud enough for all to hear. The comments came from a fifty-year-old deacon sitting two rows directly behind me. He was a faithful member and considered to be a "good" man, but was also known as a "hothead." I knew he harbored deep-seated prejudice.

"I don't know why we want this property. It'll just be filled with a bunch of . . ." And, he used an ugly and coarse racial word. One more time, as the report continued, he used the same degrading term and everyone was silent. The third time he used the term I stood up, pointed my finger directly at him, called him by name and said, "That is not proper language for a Christian much less a deacon."

He came up out of his seat and lunged for me. Deacons and chairs scattered like a bar room fight. I didn't move and watched as some of the deacons reacted quickly enough to block him from reaching me until he cooled down. Somehow order was restored. Needless to say, this display placed a rather negative spirit over the discussion of the piece of property. In fact, the church never made the purchase. After the meeting, I was at the drinking fountain outside the meeting room trying to process what had just happened. The deacon lamely apologized for his outburst toward me during the meeting. As far as I know, he never apologized for the words that came out of his mouth or for the prejudice in his heart.

The incident disappeared into the silence about the taboo subject of race and its ugly face. Silence protected the decorum and sanctity of the deacons meeting. I'm not sure if the deacons even shared the incident with their wives. Some of the deacons were supportive of my efforts to apply Christian teachings to race relations in the community. However, one or two probably supported the deacon who came after me. The other deacons were in the large and silent middle. Nevertheless, everyone was embarrassed by the spectacle of a deacon wanting to fight the pastor in a Deacon's Meeting. Most just wished the conflict would go away. I felt at the time that some of the deacons were more embarrassed by the angry exchange than the ugly racial words. Only one deacon spoke directly to me about the incident although several supported me silently.

The "White Brother"

Dick approached me early the next Sunday morning as I was entering the church offices. Dick was an older deacon who was progressive about the race issue. He wanted to encourage me about what had happened in the Deacon's Meeting and about the racial tension in the community and church. Dick counseled caution and patience about the race issue. "Preacher, these things take time. Some of us who are old and set in our ways will have to die before this changes." I responded, "Dick, this attitude is not right and we should change it now." I added, "And one day Dick when you stand before the Lord you are going to understand how wrong it is for us to refuse to speak out on this issue!"

While in the Birmingham City Jail, Martin Luther King, Jr. wrote a letter to a group of white clergymen who had written a public letter calling for patience. In his response to the clergymen, Dr. King recalls a letter he received "from a white brother in Texas." Dick could have been that "white brother" who wrote: "All Christians know that the colored people will receive equal rights eventually, but it is possible that you are in too great a religious hurry. It has taken Christianity almost two thousand years to accomplish what it has. The teachings of Christ take time to come to earth.'"

Dr. King responded: "Such an attitude stems from a tragic misconception of time, from the strangely irrational notion that there is something in the very flow of time that will inevitably cure all ills. Actually, time itself is neutral; it can be used either destructively or constructively. More and more I feel that the people of ill will have used time much more effectively than have the people of good will. We will have to repent in this generation not merely for the hateful words and actions of the bad people but for the appalling silence of the good people. Human progress never rolls in on wheels of inevitability; it comes through the tireless efforts of men willing to be co-workers with God, and without this hard work, time itself becomes an ally of the forces of social stagnation. We must use time creatively, in the knowledge that the time is always ripe to do right. Now is the time to make real the promise of democracy and transform our pending national elegy into a creative psalm of brotherhood. Now is the time to lift our national policy from the quicksand of racial injustice to the solid rock of human dignity." In fact, Dr. King often used the quote from a Supreme Court decision: "Justice delayed is justice denied."

Several months after my conversation with Dick, I left that church to be a missionary in Thailand. During my first year in Thailand, I received word that Dick had died of a heart attack. My first thought was "Dick is with the Lord." My second thought was: "Dick, now you see the full picture. Now you know about the limit of God's patience in the face of intolerance and injustice."

Why Do Some Act and Others Remain Silent?

STORY 25

"Ordinary" Ethics: A Birthday Party

*History will have to record that the greatest
tragedy of this period of social transition was
not the strident clamor of the bad people, but
the appalling silence of the good people.*
Martin Luther King Jr.
December 3, 1959

A birthday party for our seven-year old twins presented me with a difficult moral and social choice. My own courage and integrity were put to the test because Joey and Jimmy wanted to invite Ricky to their overnight birthday party. Ricky was one of their best friends at school and Ricky was Black. Theoretically, I knew what to do about inviting Ricky to the birthday party. I had preached about it. However, doing what I knew was correct proved to be a far more difficult decision than preaching about it. I learned that even the most "ordinary" ethical decisions are always made in a context and with consequence. Mary never hesitated about inviting Ricky and the twins didn't seem to sense any problem. However, I began to personally count the cost.

I was pastor of the Baptist Church in town and we lived in the parsonage that stood adjacent to the Church building on Main Street. Jefferson was the County Seat of the last county in the State of Texas to integrate its public-school system. The County was 65% Black to 35% White and the town was evenly divided between the two races.

The past decade had witnessed much turmoil in the South. A daily dose of news reported bus boycotts, Freedom Marches, attack dogs, fire hoses breaking up peaceful demonstrations, "sit-ins" at Woolworths and forced integration of schools. Tensions were high, emotions were hot and actions were ugly. Three civil rights workers were killed during this time period while engaging in voter registration in Mississippi. The events were later depicted in the movie *Mississippi Burning*. Dr. Martin Luther King and other Civil Rights leaders had been attacked, arrested, put in jail and threatened. Dr. King had given his now famous "I Have a Dream" speech on the Mall in Washington. He was assassinated in Memphis in 1969, the year after I became pastor of the Church. My "ordinary" birthday party took place the summer after the first year of the integration of our Public Schools.

Every time I mentioned the "race" issue from the pulpit, there were consequences. The only reason I survived those difficult days was because a number of my members had influence in the church, school system, and town and protected me from being fired. Several nights I went to sleep thinking some of the racist county thugs might burn a cross on the front lawn of the parsonage.

At the time of the birthday crisis, the town was in the throes of great emotion and fear. That is why our twins had Ricky as their best friend. The integration of the public-school system had put Joey, Jimmy and Ricky together. Joey and Jimmy didn't know Ricky was considered to be different by the culture of that area. They just liked Ricky.

The Birthday Party

This was the context for my difficult ethical decision about an "ordinary" birthday party. The dilemma was that this ordinary birthday party was happening during extraordinary and even potentially dangerous times. Many expedient questions began to battle within me.

"Is inviting Ricky to the birthday party worth risking the possible negative reaction?"

"Is the benefit worth the possible consequences?"

"If I am fired over this, won't it harm all the wonderful good I am trying to do in the community about race relations?"

"What difference can it really make if Ricky is discretely excluded?"

"Will Ricky even know the reason he isn't invited?"

"Will the twins really be that disappointed if I explain a little of the situation to them about the real world?"

I agonized over this ordinary birthday decision for several reasons, some more honorable than others. This innocent little party challenged the social, culture, and political institutions of the town, and it challenged whether I truly believed what I preached. Inviting Ricky to the birthday party could also affect the economic well-being of my family because I really thought I was walking on the razors edge of being fired.

Finally, I decided I could not be a hypocrite with my children. I could not teach the value that every human is equally important and deny that value by refusing to allow my sons to invite their friend to their birthday party. I had to try to practice what I preached, no matter the cost. I could not preach in the pulpit what I wasn't willing to live out in my family.

Ricky came to the party, stayed the night with all the other children and I did not hear any repercussions. I breathed a sigh of relief and devoted my time trying to put out some of the other fires that were flaming during that volatile time and place.

Ordinary Ethics Do Matter

We left that Church in 1974 and went to Thailand when our twin sons were ten years old, our third son, Matt was five and our daughter, Juleigh, was three. Almost thirty years after the birthday party, we were living in Houston. Mary received a call from a man who asked if we were the Beckham family who had lived in Jefferson during the late 1960s and early 1970s. It was Ricky. He had tracked us down. With great emotion, Ricky shared that our family had been "one of the most important things in his life during that time." Mary got his phone number and Joey and Jimmy called Ricky.

He didn't mention the birthday party. However, I now know my decision and attitude about that birthday party had something to do with Ricky's life, and mine. I now understand the importance of being true to values even in (and maybe especially in) "ordinary" situations. This was more than a birthday party that affected one little boy. It was an ethical principle and life value that related to me, a family, a church, a town, a State, a Nation, and God.

Looking back, I have several reactions. I am thrilled that the simple kindness touched Ricky's life. I also feel a degree of embarrassment because doing the right thing in what should have been an ordinary situation was such an agonizing decision. I look back at this with great fear. What if God had not helped me see with my eyes, hear with my ears, feel with my heart and touch with my life this one little boy?

This reminds me that there is no such thing as an ordinary injustice. I must always be vigilant to speak and act in the face of injustice, no matter how ordinary the situation may appear.

CONCLUSION

THE NATURE OF SILENCE

Silence gives consent.
Oliver Goldsmith

Silence is a central element in each of the stories in this little book. My exploration of the heart of man in the ethical decision-making process has constantly led me back to my original question:

In the face of injustice why do some act and others remain silent?

Why do some look the other way and others sacrifice life and property to right the wrongs being committed?

I began this book with a chapter about how silence contributes to injustice and suffering. I want to conclude with thoughts about the nature of silence.

The word "silence" fits into a group of generally appealing words such as quietness, tranquility, stillness, calm, hush, serenity and peacefulness. In one sense, silence is golden.

Muhammad Ali, a person recognized for his verbal as well as boxing skills, said "Silence is golden . . . . when you can't think of a good answer."

Someone has said: "Silence is more musical than any song."

Seneca wrote in the 1st Century: "It is a great thing to know the season for speech and the season for silence."

William Penn defined true silence as "the rest of the mind; it is to the spirit what sleep is to the body: nourishment and refreshment."

Poet Edward H. Richards praises the value of silence in his poem for children.

> *A wise old owl sat on an oak;*
> *The more he saw the less he spoke;*
> *The less he spoke the more he heard;*
> *Why aren't we like that wise old bird?*

Silence also has a spiritual dimension. The Bible encourages us to relate to God in quietness, stillness and silence.

> *A fool is thought wise if he keeps silent.*
> (Proverbs 17:28.)
> *Let all the earth be silent before Him.*
> (Habakkuk 2:20.)
> *Be still before the Lord and wait patiently for him.*
> (Psalm 37:7.)
> *Be silent before me, you islands.* (Isaiah 41:1)

The Old Testament Prophet Elijah's personal experience in hearing God took place in the quietness of a "gentle blowing."

> *Go forth, and stand on the mountain before the Lord.'*
> *And behold, the Lord was passing by! And a great and strong wind was rending the mountains and breaking in pieces the rocks before the Lord; but the Lord was not in the wind. And after the wind an earthquake, but the Lord was not in the earthquake. And after the earthquake a fire, but the Lord was not in the fire; and after the fire a sound of a gentle blowing. And it came about when Elijah heard it, that he wrapped his face in his mantle, and went out and stood in the entrance of the cave. And behold, a voice came to him and said,*
> *"What are you doing here, Elijah."*
> (1 Kings 19:9-13.)

The Dark Side of Silence

Clearly though, we see a dark side to silence as well. It is this dark and ugly side of silence in these stories that most concerns me. In history, the silence of individuals, Christians, and the Church in the face of social injustice reveals an appalling indifference and callousness toward the hurts and needs of people. Far too often, the self-serving silence of the timid majority allows the angry and abusive shouts and actions of the oppressor and bully to control the history of human relationships.

This dark side of silence is the fruit of human ethical deafness, dumbness, blindness, numbness and deadness. Silence becomes the partner of the sin of omission when a person fails to do what he should do.

Silence is a subtle but powerful temptation and an almost automatic human response to social injustice. This kind of silence is the result of fear, indifference, selfishness and ignorance and produces the fruit of hypocrisy, prejudice, self-righteousness, injustice, deceit and death. The dark side of silence is the natural sanctuary and habitat of the soul that observes social injustice from a safe and insulated vantage point, detached from the human misery and suffering.

Silence is a major tool of Satan that increases the intensity of suffering and injustice and obstructs holy and ethical living. Personal silence in the face of social wrongs is a primary cause of much of the injustice and suffering in the world. This dark side of silence is one of Satan's most effective weapons to discredit the Church, the Christian and ultimately God.

The Ugly Sides of Silence

Expediency is an ugly side of silence. It is easier to "go along in order to get along." The idea is "don't rock the boat." "Don't stir up more snakes than you can kill." Martin Luther King lived through the ugliness of expediency when political leaders continued to counsel waiting and caution. "If we claim to be Christians, there is no room for expediency." (Dietrich Bonhoeffer, p25, Memoir, *The Cost of Discipleship*.)

Cowardice is an ugly side of silence. Sometimes "silence is not golden . . . just yellow." Silence can be cowardice with an acceptable public face. Cowards use silence as a shield against potential danger. Silence has a dark side when it is the product of the fear of being exposed to criticism. Abraham Lincoln concluded: "To sin by silence when they ought to protest makes cowards of men."

Selfishness is an ugly aspect of silence. I am consumed with my own needs and am silent about any situation that might threaten my convenience or wellbeing. It benefits me to remain silent. It makes sense to "keep my mouth shut" when a matter doesn't directly pertain to me. It is logical to "mind my own business" when speaking out has little or no personal upside but much downside. Therefore, silence is a shield that I can use to protect myself from involvement, exposure or expenditure of emotional energy. Silence in the face of injustice is a disease of selfishness that eats away at the soul and hardens the heart. Selfishness says emphatically "I am ***not*** my Brother's keeper!"

Consent with injustice and evil is an ugly side of silence. Oliver Goldsmith rightly points out: "Silence gives consent." The shirt Ivy wore on the plane ride I mentioned in the introduction, "Silence is Violence" . . . . . is true! Silence is dangerous because it gives permission for injustice to go unchallenged. Silence then sucks me into the sins that it has permitted and multiplies even greater evil. Therefore, silence carries a subtle but sure penalty of collective guilt. In the eyes of God my silence ties me to the resulting injustice that it allows.

Ignorance is an ugly side of silence. Some have said, "ignorance is bliss." Sadly ignorance is often embraced in order to escape unpleasant realities.

Ignorance often says, "I don't know there is injustice because I don't want to know." I am ignorant of unfairness or inequity and blind to injustice. I am convinced intellectually that a certain act is correct and choose to be ignorant of the human consequences. This accounts for the zealous justification of slavery and Nazism. Looking back in hindsight, blind ignorance that allows silence is ugly and inexplicable, but in its context and to those invested in the argument, silence seems logical and even wise. "We didn't know" is often *not* a statement about knowledge of the facts but an admission of a fear to know the facts!

Self-deception is an ugly side of silence. "The cruelest lies are often told in silence." (Robert Louis Stevenson.) I choose to believe a lie or to allow a lie. I convince myself that to remain silent in the face of injustice is prudent, wise and justified.

Hypocrisy is an ugly side of silence. Jessie Owens won four gold medals at the 1936 Olympics and was the greatest athlete of his day. One of the other black athletes was Mack Robinson, the older brother of Jackie Robinson who broke the color barrier in Major League Baseball in 1947.

The victories of the black athletes on the American Olympic Team seriously discredited Hitler's philosophy of Aryan superiority that claimed the superiority of a certain type of the white race and the inferiority of other races. However, Owens experienced the hypocrisy of silent injustice when he returned to the United States. He could not sit in the front of a bus, use a public toilet, eat in a "white" restaurant or sleep in a "white" hotel.

Owens angered many when he observed: "I wasn't invited to shake hands with Hitler in Berlin but I wasn't invited to the White House to shake hands with the President either." This statement is so devastating that some critics question its authenticity and say Owens made it up later. My feeling and experience is that if Owens did not actually encounter a snub from the White House, the scenario he depicted was certainly true.

Indifference is an ugly side of silence that is an affront to God and poison to the human soul. I don't see you. I don't hear you. I don't feel your hurts. Therefore, I am not responsible for you. Neutrality is the silent voice that says: "you are not worthy of my attention or my voice." You are a non-person, a part of the landscape. Just a machine that exists to provide a functioning service, like a car wash or vending machine. I don't see *YOU*, I just see what you **DO** to serve me.

Self-imposed deafness is an ugly side of silence. "The problem may not be silence but deafness." (*Hearing God's Voice*, Blackaby, page 25.) A tree falls in the forest and there is no living ear to hear. Was there a sound? The implication of this philosophical puzzle is that an ear is necessary to make a sound a sound. Yet, the truth is, in the midst of injustice, God is speaking and those who receive injustice are crying out. The issue is not God's voice or the cry of the weak and oppressed, often the issue is our ear. We have chosen deafness to the voices. Jesus pointed it out this way, "He that has ears to hear, let him hear."

Do Justice, Love Kindness, Walk Humbly

God gave a simple formula for the "sins of silence" to the prophet Micah. "He has told you, O man, what is good; and what does the Lord require of you but to do justice, to love kindness, and to walk humbly with your God?" (Micah 6:8 NASB).

Do justice! Be fair and treat everyone as equal.

Love kindness! Kindness may be the central quality of God. The Hebrew language tied two words together in one beautiful word "*hesed*": loving and kindness.

Walk humbly! Humility neutralizes arrogance and superiority that feeds injustice and prejudice.

As I have read about injustice in history, have lived in times of injustice, have allowed my own insensitivity to be silence and as I see injustice today, I want to cry out:

Where is the fairness?

Where is the love and kindness?

Where is the humility?

Imagine how events could have been different in the two periods of history from which these stories come if these simple principles had been applied. Imagine if people in the far and near past had done justice, loved kindness and walked humbly with God.

Then, imagine what would happen if you and I follow God's formula for justice today. I believe this is our hope as we are tempted to remain silent:

Do justice!

Love kindness!

Walk humbly with God!

Ultimately, my passionate desire is that the stories in this book open our ears to the cries of social suffering around us; heal some of the social deafness that afflicts us, give us a voice to speak to social injustice, and enlarge our heart to defend the hurting and helpless.

The question we are all left with is this:

How can these stories inspire me to act as an agent for Good in the midst of injustices that I encounter today?